Hanging Sam

Maj. Gen. Samuel T. Williams, commanding general of the Twenty-fifth Infantry Division, South Korea, 1952.

Hanging Sam

A Military Biography
of General
Samuel T. Williams

From Pancho Villa to Vietnam

By Col. Harold J.
"Jack" Meyer

UNIVERSITY OF NORTH TEXAS PRESS, DENTON

E
745
W54
M48
1990

Design: Kennedy Poyser
Production: Jessie Dolch

The paper used in this book meets the minimum requirements
of the American National Standard for Permanence of
Paper for Printed Library Materials, Z39.48.1984.
Binding materials have been chosen for durability.

Library of Congress Cataloging-in-Publication Data

Meyer, Harold J., 1922–
Hanging Sam: a military biography of General Samuel T. Williams
from Pancho Villa to Vietnam / by Harold J. Meyer.
Includes bibliographical references and index.
ISBN 0-929398-12-2
1. Williams, S. T. (Samuel Tankersley), 1897–1984. 2. Generals—
United States—Biography. 3. United States. Army—Biography.
4. United States—History, Military—20th century. I. Title.
E745.W54M48 1990
335'.0092—dc20
[B]   90-35952   CIP

Contents

Illustrations

Preface

The task of biographers is simplified if they have had personal contact with their subjects. Thus, I have found it easier to write some of the pages that follow because I served under (not *with*) Colonel Samuel Tankersley Williams in Bamberg, Germany, from May 1949 until mid-1950, at which time he returned stateside to an assignment with Army Field Forces at Fort Monroe, Virginia.

May Day 1949 found me—a second lieutenant, infantry—railroading from Bremerhaven to Bad Tölz, Germany, where the First Infantry Division headquarters was located. There, I reported to Lt. Col. George D. Patterson. During the interview he asked me if I intended to make the army my career.

"Yes sir," I replied.

"In that case," Colonel Patterson said, "I am going to assign you to 'Hanging Sam' and his Blue Spaders."

Those were strange identifications to me, and I queried, "Hanging Sam? Blue Spaders?"

Colonel Patterson smiled and answered, "Colonel Samuel T. Williams and his Twenty-sixth Infantry Regiment. Both are located in Bamberg, Germany." He continued, "It appears that you want to be a career army officer. This is why I am going to assign you to the finest colonel of infantry in Germany and our entire army, in my judgment. He is a well-decorated officer who has demonstrated his personal courage and convictions numerous times. If you survive his military mentorship, your future will be assured. I wish you good luck, Lieutenant Meyer, for you will need it under Sam."

During the months that followed, I never spoke to Colonel Williams except socially. A full schedule of training kept my attention; every minute of my eighty-hour duty week was directed toward professional development. Rigorous training was followed by more physically and mentally demanding field maneuvers. Colonel Williams could be seen (preferably through binoculars at long range), but the rank and organizational distance between a lieutenant and a colonel limited personal contact. Yet that first year with the Blue Spaders was profitable for me because under Colonel Williams I became aware of the significance of goals and the importance of unit training, competition, small unit leadership, dedication to the army, and the development of esprit de corps. He set the pace, and we hurried to keep up with him.

But I learned little about Colonel Williams in those days of 1949–50. We troops and young officers of the Blue Spaders knew nothing of his relief and reduction in August of 1944 from brigadier general to colonel. We knew little about his Texas background, his superb devotion to duty, and unquestioned loyalty to his superiors even under the most trying of professional circumstances. Nor were we aware of his obsession to regain his lost military stature.

When General Williams retired in 1960, after more than forty-four years of faithful service in the United States Army, he wore the three stars of a lieutenant general on his shoulder. He had "come back."

To have served with him as a subordinate or as a senior was for some a challenge and for others a career disaster. He demanded the keenest military performance from those assigned to his unit; nothing but professional perfection would satisfy him. He caused ulcers, mid-career burnout, heart attacks, divorces, and the resignations of commissioned officers of the regular army. But he never swerved from achieving the mission assigned to him and his unit. Nor did he ever, after his reduction, set aside or forget his drive to be a general officer again.

As the manuscript developed, a nagging question arose in my mind: Why? Why did Gen. Omar N. Bradley approve the recommendations of a corps and a division commander to reduce Brig. Gen. Samuel T. Williams? My research failed to reveal facts that Sam's combat performance and professional demeanor warranted Bradley's severe punishment. Based on my study of the material and the evidence available to me, I conclude with deep conviction that General Bradley was disloyal and unfair to General Williams in July of 1944. But Sam survived this devastating blow with dignity and the absence of ill will because he was a soldier, from the day he joined the Texas Militia in 1916 to the day he retired in 1960.

This book is about Sam—a soldier.

☆   ☆   ☆

A word of advice to those readers who may look here for disclosures that point to the origins of or reasons for the various military conflicts that Sam Williams participated in: read no further. This book is about a Texan who found his realm in the 1916 world of '03 rifles, Pancho Villa, campaign hats, khaki clothing, military bugle calls, and the certainty of coming war. I do not discuss those national affairs that carried Sam Williams to Germany, Korea, or Vietnam unless his career raised the matter. If what I have discovered assisted me in telling his story, I have included it. Every chapter has been developed and written through my own tunnel vision, and this vision has focused on Sam Williams.

Col. Harold J. "Jack" Meyer
U.S. Army, Retired
Destin, Florida

Acknowledgments

As a novice biographer, I sought and received information from many people eager to share their knowledge with me of Lt. Gen. Samuel T. Williams. I have been given valuable aid from professional historians, World War II buffs, scholars, and archivists. Sergeants and general officers and aides-de-camp have enlightened me about my subject, and I interviewed members of several U.S. Army division associations. I have written hundreds of letters and received hundreds of replies from correspondents who told me what they knew about Sam. Reminiscences contributed by several correspondents who asked to remain anonymous were used in the manuscript only after they were authenticated by less shy respondents. Many of Sam's former close associates offered choice tidbits of fact to help make the work precise and accurate.

The varied recollections of the Williams family also proved to be invaluable; they contributed so much to Sam's personality and character. To them, I express a particular word of recognition and gratitude. Their names as contributors are mentioned elsewhere, as are the names of those who gave of their time and talents to help me develop this effort.

One of the most difficult challenges I faced in gathering information was presented by the National Personnel Records Center in St. Louis. General Williams left no descendants and his spouse was deceased when my research began. The NPRC insisted that I would have to present a certified paper from the next-of-kin before they would consider opening the Williams file to me. For more than a year, the NPRC bureaucracy defeated me despite the provisions of the Freedom of Information Act and the Privacy Act, both of 1974. When I finally received the Lt. Gen. Samuel T. Williams records, it was because of the efforts of the executor of the Williams estate, not because of my frontal attacks.

As the wealth of information about Sam grew, it became obvious that I would have to consider other sources in order to put the Sam Williams story in proper perspective. It was necessary to reinforce and balance the garnered information with official and unofficial histories, private manuscripts, and Sam's personal papers. I studied these related materials at the National Archives, Washington, D.C.; the U.S. Army Military History Institute, Carlisle Barracks, Pennsylvania; the technical libraries of the U.S. Army Command and General Staff College, Fort Leavenworth, Kansas; and the U.S. Army Infantry School, Fort Benning, Georgia. In order to gain an appreciation for the terrain above Utah beach on the Normandy coast, I visited the battlefields there of the Ninetieth Infantry Division.

Should error be discovered despite the extensive research, the flaw remains mine alone. Mistakes that come to light are due to my research frailties and are not included intentionally. Also, my interpretation of facts may differ from that of some readers.

I am indebted to the following for their submissions, persuasive powers, and keen insights into the character of Sam Williams. The names are not in any particular order; each contribution was important—the shortest equaling the longest. I extend my appreciation to each with a sincere word of thanks: Col. Norman H. Bykerk; Maj. Gen. Charles C. Case; Mr. O. Scott Petty; Mr. Patrick H. Reagan; Mr. Charles C. Spear; Richard J. Sommers; Lt. Col. Eames L. Yates; Lt. Col. Peter A. Dul; Mr. Carl Everett; Col. Richard Cross; Maj. Gen. Fred E. Karhohs; Lt. Col. Boyd F. Reeder; Col. Charles R. Wright; Col. Frank S. Plummer; Lt. Col. Don Rivette; Gen. James M. Gavin; Mr. and Mrs. Herbert Harris; Mrs. W.B. Keusseff; Mrs. George J. Merriman; Mr. John F. Shea; Command Sgt. Maj. Ted Dobol; Mr. and Mrs. Henri Levaufre; Mr. and Mrs. Guy Blondel; Lt. Col. Edward S.

Hamilton; Mr. William J. Falvey; Col. Carl C. Ulsaker; Gen. William DePuy; Gen. Richard G. Stilwell; Gen. Orwin C. Talbott; Gen. Maxwell D. Taylor; Lt. Gen. Edward A. Partain; Brig. Gen. Francis A. Woolfley; Col. Nathaniel P. Ward III; Brig. Gen. Edwin Van V. Sutherland ; Col. Erwin G. Nilsson; Mr. Carl W. Manuel; and Lt. Jack Moyer.

Photographs are courtesy of the U.S. Army, National Archives, Mrs. Mitzi Canfield, Lt. Col. Peter Dul, Mr. Richard Harris, Mr. Woodson Harris, Mr. Charles Spear, and Lt. Col. Eames Yates.

Finally, there is one important name missing in the foregoing. It is that of my spouse of more than forty-four years—Celes'. Her encouragement and patience throughout the days of travel, research, and writing have been limitless. Celes' has been understanding, supportive, and the best of critics. Her humor served us both well.

(Above) Lt. Gen. Samuel T. Williams, Ft. Sam Houston, 1955.

(Next page) The Ninetieth Infantry Division, with Brig. Gen. Samuel T. Williams as its assistant division commander, was on board the Susan B. Anthony *when it sank off the Normandy coast on June 7, 1944. All 2,400 troops were safely evacuated under General Williams' leadership.*

AP 72
PORT BOW VIEW
NORFOLK NAVY YARD
PHOTO SERIAL 5248(43) MAY 13, 1943

Chapter 1 ☆ ☆ ☆ *The* Susan B. Anthony

Brig. Gen. Samuel Tankersley Williams, United States Army, stood straight as a colonial rifle on the antiaircraft deck of the U.S. Navy transport *Susan B. Anthony.* From there, high above the bridge, he scanned the faintly visible horizon to the south that was disturbed by the flickering silhouettes of hundreds of ships of every configuration: corvettes, gunboats, destroyers, battleships, antisubmarine craft, plus LSTs and LCIs, which were easy to identify. Unseen by General Williams was the enemy-held coast of Normandy, the objective of the forces wallowing in the murky waters of the English Channel.

It was Wednesday, D-day+1, 7 June 1944.

General Williams was the assistant division commander of the Ninetieth Infantry Division—the "Tough Ombres," as it was known to its members. It was also called the TO outfit because many of its men—the riflemen, tankers, cannon-cockers, engineers, and quartermasters—were proud to be from Texas or Oklahoma. Sam shared their pride of origin, for he was a Texan, born in Denton, Texas, the son of Darwin Herbert and Ida Cessna Williams.

At the moment, he was a forty-seven-year-old one-star army general at sea off Portland, England, with the leading advance forces of the Ninetieth. Aboard the *Anthony*, in addition to the forward combat element, were others of the Ninetieth, such as the Second Battalion of the 359th Infantry Regiment, the division Signal Company, and medics and reconnaissance units. In all, the *Susan B. Anthony* was loaded with 2,400 soldiers and officers of the division, all of whom, along with weapons and equipment, were moving toward the north shore of France—and war.

The *Susan B. Anthony*, once known as the *Santa Clara*, was launched in 1930 and served as a cruise ship for eleven years. But in 1942, the ship was refitted and commissioned for duty as a navy troop transport. Capable of carrying more than 2,500 soldiers and most of their equipment for a range of 9,000 miles with its electro-turbine engines and nineteen knots of speed, the *Anthony* could outrun the swiftest Nazi submarine. It was one-and-one-half football fields long, sixty-three feet wide, and comfortable in as little as twenty-five feet of water. Capt. Thomas A. Grey knew the ship well because he had also served as its captain when it sailed the commercial pleasure routes off California and the waters of the Pacific. The *Susan B. Anthony* was an experienced vessel with a qualified crew and skipper.

The Ninetieth Motorized Division was activated at Camp Barkley, Texas, in March of 1942, with Maj. Gen. Henry Terrell assigned as its first World War II commander. Terrell was acclaimed as one of the best trainers in the U.S. Army and held an enviable reputation as a competent soldier and leader, but he left the Ninetieth in January of 1944 as it prepared for overseas shipment at Fort Dix, New Jersey.

Terrell's replacement was Brig. Gen. Jay W. MacKelvie, who enlisted in the army in January of 1913 and was within three years the sergeant major of the Seventh Cavalry Regiment—a remarkable achievement for a newly enlisted soldier. He continued to advance and was commissioned in the Regular Army as a second lieutenant, artillery, in June of 1917. In August he was promoted to captain. After being commissioned, MacKelvie was ordered to Camp Logan, Texas, where he joined the Seventy-eighth Field Artillery. Shortly thereafter he sailed to Europe with the Twenty-eighth Field Artillery and participated in the St. Mihiel offensive.

After his return to the United States, his assignments were routine, highlighted with attendance at the army's Command and General Staff School in 1932. Four years later, he graduated from the Army War College. Between the schooling years, he continued to master the science of artillery.

In February of 1942 he joined the Plans Group of the War Plans Division, War Department General Staff. There, he became known to Chief of Staff General George C. Marshall, who selected him to become artillery commander of the Eighty-fifth Infantry Division stationed at Camp Shelby, Mississippi. In September of 1943 he was further recognized as a skilled artillery officer when Marshall directed him to assume command of the XII Corps Artillery located at Fort Bragg, North Carolina.

Four months later, MacKelvie became commanding general of the Ninetieth while still wearing his single silver star. His khaki shirt collar would never sport a second one.

Sam needed no introduction to General MacKelvie because they had met in 1936 at Fort Benning, Georgia. At that time, it had been *Captain* Williams and *Major* MacKelvie. By 1944 at Fort Dix, both were brigadier generals, but MacKelvie was senior to Williams by nearly a year, so it was "General MacKelvie" and "Sam."

Sam arranged briefings for MacKelvie that touched on every unit of the division, and he personally introduced him to key personnel no matter their rank or title. Throughout the orientation, Sam underscored the status of training and emphasized those matters that General Terrell had found important, plus the findings of inspectors who had accompanied them on maneuvers in Arizona, Texas, and Louisiana. Sam also told MacKelvie of his concern about the quality of the replacements being received for the original Tough Ombres who were found unqualified for overseas duty.

Throughout the orientation, MacKelvie remained aloof and generally made little comment. He became known to the Ninetieth general staff as "Oral Non."

Sam maintained a formal military posture with MacKelvie—proper, polite, and not the least familiar. MacKelvie for his part immediately began to influence the division by applying what seemed to be petty rules. Officers were instructed when and how to report to him and what uniforms to wear. He isolated himself from his staff. Officer morale in particular began to unravel when MacKelvie took charge of the Ninetieth Infantry Division at Fort Dix.

As Sam tried to familiarize MacKelvie with the overall situation of the division, he was also preparing to depart to England to await the division's arrival. With the assistance of the Ninetieth's chief of staff, Sam selected a group of leaders to accompany him to England, choosing officers and enlisted technicians in whom he had confidence—those whom he knew fulfilled the requirements of coordination, command, and communications that would be needed in England.

After arriving there in March of 1944, Sam moved to the Birmingham area and began to establish camps for the division. The division's continued training was essential and primary to all else for Sam.

During World War II, an assistant division commander normally was expected to concern himself with the training of the division's members, but especially with the infantry soldiers. Sam later wrote that "during our stay in England, I had little opportunity to carry out this important duty."[1] Most of Sam's attention on the arrival of the Ninetieth was spent at VII Corps headquarters developing plans for the Tough Ombres' combat role. The division would contribute one regiment—the 359th—to the initial landing force. The 359th, less its Second Battalion, was attached to the Fourth Infantry Division, which was scheduled to land at daybreak on Monday, June 5th.

The 359th Infantry Regiment would return to MacKelvie's control after the entire Ninetieth was marshalled south of Utah beach. The plan then directed the Ninetieth, along with the Fourth Division, to move to the northwest to participate in the capture of the vital Cherbourg port as part of the VII Corps.

In a letter to his sister Ida, written 18 January 1963, Sam wrote:

I did not endear myself to some of my superiors because of my objections to various things that were planned or being done. I knew the German soldier from personal experience, for I had fought them at the platoon and company level. I knew that the German soldier could and would fight to the last ditch, if ordered to do so, regardless of what our higher command thought about the German Army.

For example, the original landing plans had us (the 90th) land on the beach with the 4th and capture the port of Cherbourg, some miles to our west, in four days.

My objections and undoubtedly the objections of others, caused the time limit to be extended to 14 days. At any rate, as it turned out, Cherbourg was not captured in 14 days; it was close to twenty and it took three (not two) divisions to do it.

Cherbourg fell to the combined strength of the Fourth, Ninth, and the Seventy-ninth Divisions on June 26th, twenty days after the first American soldier waded ashore at Utah beach. Other planning that occupied Sam related to detailed arrangements for the on-loading of ships for crossing the English Channel, as well as the rapid off-loading of landing craft and military transports on-and-off the beach.

Sam was not satisfied with what he discovered at the transportation headquarters in London, although he managed to have additional ships assigned to the Ninetieth plus three experienced British officers—a navy captain and two marine officers. Their attention, as well as Sam's, was given to every aspect of loading and unloading personnel and equipment. Sam later credited the British officers with much of the success of the embarkation and debarkation of the vessels, which followed a last-on first-off plan.

The *Susan B. Anthony* was completely loaded at Cardiff by midday 3 June 1944. Sam observed the final loading and, surprisingly, he offered little criticism or comment. Typically, he was looking forward to the next major activity of the operation—getting the ship unloaded with the same efficiency that characterized the loading.

After boarding the *Anthony*, Sam moved to the AA deck, where he could be found during most of the voyage south to Swansea and on to mid-Channel. One senior officer said that General Williams feared seasickness and therefore purposely detached himself from the main flow of shipboard traffic. More likely, he wanted to be at the center of activity in case of air attack, although such a challenge by enemy aircraft was improbable. Yet he was aware that the *Anthony* was a lucrative target.

About the movement to Swansea, Sam wrote:

> From the moment we boarded, it was pleasant. The soldiers were not crowded or uncomfortable. While the water was heavy and running with long rolls, the ship rode with smoothness. The weather was similar to what we had known in Wales. The food was outstanding for our Army menu in the Isles was not so generous with steak, butter, eggs and fresh baked bread. The soldiers, as usual, made remarks about this, "Our Last Supper." We had no sooner departed the sight of land and were in the Bristol Channel when I heard dice rolling and cards being shuffled.
> Of course, we got some soldiering done. We hung cargo nets for practice in lowering ourselves to the decks of our pick-up craft. Abandon boat drills were held. I held discussions with our naval representatives to learn from their experiences what to look for when debarking troops.[2]

The plans for the invasion called for shore landings on Monday, June 5th, but the weather in the Channel and along the coast of France delayed the adventure. The *Susan B. Anthony* and other ships of the Ninetieth would remain at anchor until the early evening of June 5th, with D-day scheduled for the 6th.

Sam directed unit commanders aboard the *Anthony* to take advantage of the delay by conducting additional instruction.

He stressed the first priority of maintaining weapons, followed by physical training, map reading, and first aid. He also suggested that classes be again held that would teach uniform recognition, with emphasis on the American paratrooper dress as contrasted with the field gray of the German soldier.

The *Susan B. Anthony* received orders to depart Swansea at mid-evening, June 5th, along with other ships carrying Ninetieth Division units. Twenty-four hours later, she was off Portland in the English Channel where two British destroyers joined another destroyer and two destroyer escorts, all of which were to accompany the *Anthony* to anchorage off Utah.

The news of the early-morning landings on Utah, June 6th, and elsewhere in France was heartening to the soldiers. The British Broadcasting Corporation announced at 3:00 P.M. that the airborne operations were a success; many German shore batteries had been silenced, and the British were heavily engaged near Caen. A German broadcast said the attack ranged from Le Havre in the east to Cherbourg in the west. Sam persuaded the ship's master to have the news announced a second time over the public address system.

On Wednesday, June 7th, Sam was on the bridge at first light. He talked to the young naval officer in charge, and they discussed the improvement of the weather during the movement from Portland. They also discussed depth charges that escorts had dropped the evening before. Sam was happy it had occurred, "for it helped keep the troops aware of their purpose for being here in the middle of the English Channel."[3]

By 7:30 A.M., Sam had moved to the upper AA station. There he was joined by the division's chief of staff, Col. Robert L. Bacon; the G2, Lt. Col. James Boswell; his aide-de-camp, Lt. Carl Everett; and Dr. Robert D. Natchwey of the 315th Medical Battalion. All were astounded to see the vast number of ships of every description visible in all directions. Then too, they could hear faintly the distant echo of heavy detonations coming from the south. Sam remarked, "It is not unlike the explosions we became accustomed to long ago at Barkley."[4]

Other officers climbed the ladder to the AA position.

Although Sam had not called a meeting, he decided to make use of the time by reviewing the mission and the responsibilities of those who had gathered spontaneously.

But unseen, a German magnetic mine drifted upward from the channel's bottom and touched the *Susan B. Anthony*'s port stern plates deep below her waterline. Few noticed the explosion because its deadly report was muffled by the water.

The *Anthony* was mortally stricken.

At the moment of detonation, the ship's stern was exposed well above the water level. At the same time, the ship twisted and violently shook the entire length of its underwater spine. The shuddering caused rivets below decks to be propelled in every direction, each as deadly as a fired rifle bullet. They penetrated the soldiers' combat packs, drilled holes in the galley stoves, riddled equipment of every description, and punctured the mirrors and toilets of a troop bathroom.

In an instant, the ship was lifeless, quiet, and without purpose. It had lost all power and was motionless except for a little drift and a perceptible lowering of the stern and heavily damaged upper structure. The broken and distorted mast pointed to the *Anthony*'s final beach, fifty-three fathoms below.

But as the ship went silent, General Sam Williams spoke up and took charge. Quietly and firmly he ordered:

"Bacon, get a damage report, then meet me on the bridge.

"Boswell, go below, kick ass, and get the troops topside.

"Everett, assist Colonel Boswell.

"Dr. Natchwey, take care of the wounded.

"All of you, get the troops to their abandon-ship stations.

"Move out, goddam it, we are needed on the beach."

General Williams dropped to the bridge and asked Captain Grey about the situation. Grey said he could only guess as to how long the ship would remain afloat. Williams, after a quick look to the *Anthony*'s rear, passed the word for all army personnel to prepare to abandon ship.

Williams also asked Captain Grey if he would bring rescue ships alongside. Grey said that he had already taken such steps but that nearby ships had not yet recognized his signalman. In the meantime, soldiers were forming quietly as directed by their noncommissioned officers. A tug moved in and touched the *Anthony*'s port side near the stern, but Grey directed it to move to the other side because he could not abandon ship off the left. The tug cast off and moved to the starboard but immediately returned to its original position. Colonel Boswell reported to General Williams that the troops were posted at their abandon-ship positions and requested permission to evacuate the soldiers near the port side. Williams told him to do so and turned to Grey, asking him if there was any way he could beach the *Anthony* near Utah. Grey said no; the vessel was settling too rapidly. Williams directed the carrying parties to search for and recover as many weapons as possible. While this was being done, he left the bridge to personally make sure that the lower decks were clear of soldiers.

In a Recommendation for Award dated 22 June 1944, Colonel Bacon wrote, "General Williams took active charge of the evacuation of all troops and, using four members of the staff for specific inspections of holds and troop compartments, he determined that all troops were taken off; first the injured, then the advance detachment, and then other troops in order of availability as craft came alongside."

On his return from the lower decks, General Williams ordered Colonel Bacon to get the advance detachment off the ship and move to the beach, acting as the detachment's acting commander and carrying out its mission. Williams said he would stay with the ship until he was sure all the men were off of it and ordered his principal officer assistants to move the soldiers still aboard to the prow, for the ship was sinking rapidly. Williams made another quick survey below decks to ensure that all soldiers were above, forward, and abandoning ship.

Dr. Natchwey reported to General Williams that there were several casualties requiring treatment, but nothing life threatening. Later, the young medical officer wrote that his first World War II casualty was a soldier who sustained a severe gash of the right buttock—"an ignominious way," he noted, "to earn the Purple Heart for the wound was caused when the toilet on which the soldier was seated shattered as the mine exploded." Natchwey received some morphine sulphate himself to counteract the intense pain of a strained back. The doctor later said of the thirty-milligram injection that "it made scrambling down the cargo net and onto the deck of a dancing LCI a piece of cake."[5]

By 9:45, nearly all soldiers and crew had moved to rescue vessels. After ordering the remaining soldiers to evacuate, General Williams turned to Captain Grey and told him that he was leaving. He and his aide boarded the British gunboat *Nedbrough*, where he hurried to the bridge and asked the captain to direct all boats that had picked up survivors to head for Utah beach.

But the confusion, the noise, and the drab sight of the burning and sinking *Susan B. Anthony* distracted from General Williams' orders, and by 10:00 A.M., when the *Anthony* was gone, Williams and those with him on the *Nedbrough* stood offshore on Omaha beach, V Corps zone. Later, they found transport to Utah.

On 22 June 1944, the commanding general of the Ninetieth Division forwarded a Recommendation for Award letter to General Eisenhower's headquarters, recommending that General Williams be awarded the Legion of Merit. In part the letter stated, "When the U.S. Transport, *Susan B. Anthony*, struck a mine and was fatally damaged off the Carentan Peninsula, General Williams, the senior troop officer aboard, immediately took charge of the evacuation of the troops aboard the transport, and by reason of his energetic and resourceful leadership under constant danger to his own life, all the 2,400 troops aboard were safely evacuated in the one-and-one-half hours before the doomed ship sank."

But the recommendation was not favorably considered. The endorsement returning the letter to the Ninetieth stated that although the acts described were meritorious, they were insufficient to justify the award for which they were recommended.

No further attention was given to the courage and bravery of General Williams until 30 April 1945 when Maj. Gen. Ernest N. Harmon, XXII Corps commanding general, wrote to the Ninetieth Division that he believed General Williams' outstanding service during the sinking of the *Anthony* should be recognized.

He called attention to the correspondence that had been disapproved for the Legion of Merit. General Harmon mentioned that General Marshall had personally dispatched a congratulatory message to Williams. In closing his letter, General Harmon recommended that consideration be given to awarding the Soldier's Medal to Williams, which was indeed presented to him for his leadership aboard the *Susan B. Anthony* shortly after the war ended.

When the orders from the Ninetieth awarding General Williams the Soldier's Medal were received, they were addressed to Col. Samuel T. Williams. The rank used to identify Sam was correct. Gen. Omar N. Bradley, First Army commanding general, had recommended to General Eisenhower that Williams be relieved as assistant division commander, Ninetieth Infantry Division, and then reduced to the grade of colonel.

Eisenhower approved Bradley's recommendations and found General Williams' performance in combat unsatisfactory, reduced him one grade, and ordered him to leave the European theater of operations.

On 7 August 1944, exactly two months after the sinking of the *Anthony*, Colonel Williams began his journey from England to Washington, D.C.

(Above) Sam Williams around the turn of the century. Sam's father owned a photography studio in Denton, Texas.

(Next page) Future U.S. Army general Sam Williams in a casual military posture he favored even as an adult.

Chapter 2✰ ✰ ✰*Tea-Pot*

Samuel T. Williams was born 25 August 1897 in Denton, Texas. His mother was a thirty-eight-year-old housewife, and his forty-four-year-old father owned and operated the Williams Photography Studio. Although not wealthy, the family was comfortable. Sam spent most of his childhood in a house built in 1904 that remains today, a stately home located near the University of North Texas campus. His mother remained there after the death of her husband in 1918.

Mrs. Ida Cessna Williams was a strong, refined, loving mother who never swerved from her devotion to her family nor deviated from her dedication to the First Presbyterian Church or her community. The strength of her character was obvious in Sam, his oldest brother Charles, who was fifteen at the time of Sam's birth, and the two other brothers, Ed and Fred. Sam's two sisters—Ida and Mary—were popular and well-liked. None of

Sam's siblings followed him in the military profession, but Fred served in the navy during World War I and in the army during World War II.

Sam's early childhood days were undistinguished, but family members recall a particular incident that caused the young Sam great embarrassment. He had become infatuated in the second grade with Penelope Evers and had given her a card with a pretty picture on one side. On the reverse side he had written "I love you." Sam later said he regretted this childish indiscretion because his sisters teased him without mercy. "I ever after watched what I wrote and safeguarded it if necessary," Sam said.[1]

Sam began his education at the Westward School and completed it at Denton High School. He developed physically and mentally in Denton High, and although he did not hold class office during his four years there, he was an active participant in scholastic and athletic programs.

As a junior, he was invited to become a member of the Pierian Literary Society, an organization that recognized students of intellectual promise, and was selected to be the 1915–16 editor of the society's monthly newspaper, *The Flashlight*. Critics were pleased with the publication. According to Miss McCormick, the faculty adviser, it was "wonderfully gotten up."[2]

Sam was also known on the football field as Tea-Pot, an appellation said to be given to those male seniors who indicated a yearning to attend the University of Texas after high school graduation. Sam was a junior class member of the football team when he first won recognition as a guard in 1914. The coach later wrote that "Tea-pot will graduate this year [1916] and his place as guard will be hard to fill on next year's squad. Sam had plenty of grit and was always fighting. He could always be depended upon to make a hole."[3] Sam's photograph appeared in the yearbook as a Spring term graduate of 1916, and it is noted that science, bookkeeping, and football occupied his time as a student. In Sam's senior year, the Bronco football team won three games and lost three.

On 19 May 1916, sixty-four graduates walked the stage at

the Robert E. Lee Auditorium. But Sam was absent. In the early months of that year, he had become restless. He was a steady reader of Denton's newspaper, the *Record-Chronicle,* and world events were a topic of conversation at the family noon dining table, especially those that touched Texas and the United States. Sam read about a Mexican outlaw, Francisco "Pancho" Villa, who had crossed the international border between Mexico and the United States during the night of 8 March 1916. At the town of Columbus, New Mexico, he killed seven American soldiers and wounded two officers and five soldiers. Sixty-seven of the Mexican raiders were killed and seven captured. After the attack, the cavalry pursued the Mexicans some twelve miles into Mexican territory. Brig. Gen. John J. Pershing was given command of a sizable force and ordered to proceed immediately across the border and destroy the bandits who had raided Columbus. He pushed forward, scattering the bandits as he advanced. Pershing stayed in Mexico for several months, where he won a fine reputation for his handling of his forces, as well as for maintaining cordial relations with the representatives of the Mexican government and the Mexican military commanders.

Sam also read of the heightened tensions in Europe and the rivalry of the European powers that was growing between two groups—the Triple Alliance of Germany, Austria, and Hungary, plus Italy, and the Triple Entente of France, England, and Russia. Denton citizens clearly saw that war might be near at hand.

During the early months of 1916, Sam came under the influence of a local attorney, Mr. Alvin M. Owsley. In later years, Sam said that Mr. Owsley was his hero. His admiration for him was partly due to Mr. Owsley's having been a 1909 graduate of the Virginia Military Institute and its First Captain that year. After graduating from the institute, Owsley began his law education at the University of Texas and later continued it at the Laws Court in London. He was admitted to the Texas bar in 1912 while serving as a member of the Texas House of Representatives.

Earlier, Owsley had been appointed a major in the Texas Militia, and after attending a military ball in Austin, he had placed his dress blue uniform on display in a Denton clothing store window. The beautiful uniform and its owner made a considerable impression on Sam. In fact, he discussed the possibility of organizing a military unit at Denton High School, but Owsley gently pointed out in considerable detail the political and organizational ramifications of such a project. With graduation just ahead, Sam put the idea aside.

Further aggression and armed forays continued along the U.S.–Mexican border. With the presence of Mexican bandits and irregular military forces hostile to both governments, it became clear that the U.S. Army could not police it properly or assure the safety and protection of American citizens living along its edge. On 9 May 1916, President Wilson, using the authority of his office, ordered the governors of the states of Arizona, New Mexico, and Texas to activate their state militias for federal duty along the southern border or at locations deemed necessary by the commanding general of the Southern Department of the U.S. Army.

Denton did not have a National Guard company at the time; however, several young Denton men belonged to Company B, Fourth Texas Infantry, located in Fort Worth. Sam wanted to join immediately, but his parents encouraged him to graduate from high school first. Near the end of April, Sam told his parents that he intended to join the Texas Militia and that his enlistment was for six months. He would be discharged in time to enter college, which pleased his mother. She understood Sam's desire to participate in active operations against Pancho Villa along the border of Texas, but it was important to her that Sam would soon be given a "Student's Discharge," thereby permitting him to enter college.

Sam T. Williams, at the age of eighteen, enlisted in the Texas Militia near Fort Worth on 10 May 1916. Capt. Sidney W. Harrison assigned him as a private of infantry to Company B, Fourth Infantry. He was immediately sent to Fort Sam Houston, where he received military uniforms, equipment, and a rifle. Private Williams passed his physical examination without difficulty at the time of enlistment, but the examining medical officer, Maj. John A. Murtagh, wrote that Private Williams wore glasses to correct "myopia, bilateral, 20/100 each eye." He noted that "the applicant is disqualified from service in the United States Army by reason of 'defective vision.'" But he also recommended that the defect be waived because it was fully correctable with glasses.

Within hours, Sam and the other members of the company and the Fourth Infantry Regiment were moved by rail to border positions in the Big Bend area of southwestern Texas. He noted later that his regiment did not attack the Mexicans nor did the Mexicans engage the Americans during his service there.

While preparing field fortifications and digging defensive positions, Sam was also learning the art of soldiering. He was a quick learner, for he was promoted to corporal in March of 1917, and after eleven months of service, he was given the three stripes of a line sergeant.

During this time when Sergeant Williams was maturing physically and professionally as a soldier, the U.S. Army was also growing. After the nation witnessed the impotency of its forces in the forays against the Mexican bandits, Congress passed legislation to correct military deficiencies. The National Defense Act of 1916 increased the size of both the army and the National Guard. The act also provided for the creation of an organized reserve consisting of the Officers Reserve Corps and the Reserve Officers Training Corps. In 1913, at the suggestion of Maj. Gen. Leonard Wook, the War Department conducted an encampment designed to foster military discipline and encourage national preparedness. The concept was so successful that it provided for the rapid development of junior officers from volunteer sources as varied as the regular establishment, militia members, college campuses, and the business world.

War against Germany was declared 6 April 1917. When he heard the announcement that officer training camps were to be opened, Sgt. Sam Williams put his college plans aside and volunteered immediately.

(Left) Sam Williams, circa 1916. General Williams in later years would have relieved a commander for allowng a soldier to wear the frayed belt he himself wears in this photograph.

(Next page) Sam (front row, second from left) with members of his Texas Militia squad, 1916.

Chapter 3 ☆ ☆ ☆ Lt. Sam T. Williams

Resplendent in a carefully brushed and pressed uniform, Sgt. Sam T. Williams, wearing his campaign hat at a jaunty angle, appeared misplaced among the civilian volunteers who were reporting to the First Officer Training Camp at Leon Springs, Texas. Having just completed more than eleven months of hardening duty in the Big Bend area of southwestern Texas, Sergeant Williams in 1917 was bronzed from the weather and strong from his military training. He strutted confidently with measured pace among the more than three thousand civilians who arrived in early May seeking the gold bars of a second lieutenant. They were not quite as cocky as Sergeant Williams, but they too had demonstrated leadership potential, were physically fit high school graduates, and had been vouched for as men of character by three leading citizens of their community. Those who wrote in favor of Sam included his friend Maj. A.C. Owsley of Denton and the

Texas National Guard, and the Honorable George M. Hopkins, a Texas senator from Denton. The third, Capt. Sidney M. Harrison of the Fourth Texas Infantry had written in his recommendation:

> Sergeant Sam T. Williams has seen service with Company B 4th Texas Infantry since May 10, 1916 on the Mexican Border and has been a noncommissioned officer of exceptional merits and capabilities.
> The field service he has seen in connection with his previous military experience and education should give him great advantage over civilian men in training for a commission in the Reserve Officers Corp. It is with regret that I see him leave my organization. I would consider him a valuable asset to any organization to which he should become attached.[1]

Sam was spirited and obviously proud, but he also displayed traits of understanding and helpfulness to all candidates. He understood their confusion with matters military and gave of himself, as the occasion arose, to every candidate who contacted him. The volunteers from Denton received his immediate attention. The eight—Berkley E. Alexander, Joe R. Bailey, Kearie L. Berry, Homer L. Fry, Mack B. Hodges, Luther Hoffman, Menton T. Reese, and George W. Rucker—brought with them news of Denton and Denton County, but they gave their fellow North Texan little opportunity to discuss Denton because they were green, uninitiated, and eager to learn about the army and what they faced as officer candidates.

With the insight of a noncommissioned officer, Sam gave priority to their questions. He directed them to those processing areas that provided unit assignments and uniforms, and he told them where to find the mess hall. He also provided them with his camp location and gave them directions to find it.

The army semantics confused the volunteers the most. Sam told them, for instance, that it was a "mess hall," even though it was where they would eat, and sometimes what they would eat would be "slum," not stew. Also, the bathroom was a "latrine," and soldiers did not take baths, they showered; a gun would now be a "rifle" or an "03"; Sam or anyone else wearing stripes should never be called "Sarge"; the company commander should be addressed as "Captain," not the "Old Man." He also warned them that if it moved, they should salute it until they were familiar with army rank and insignia. And finally, they should trust their sergeants and listen to them, avoid the "wise asses" in their platoon, protect their belongings and money, and work hard!

Friendships among the First Campers, as they were called, endured to their deaths. Those men who remained in Sam's memory included O. Scott Petty and Gus Dittmar—who would serve with him during World War II—Walter S. Grothaus, Linton Estes, John W. McCullough, and Capt. R.T. Phinney. A tragic bombing error in France by the Army Air Corps, 25 July 1944, ended Sam's more than a quarter of a century friendship with Lt. Gen. Lesley J. McNair, who had recognized Sam's leadership potential when he was a member of the camp staff. Sam was sorely grieved when he heard of General McNair's untimely death.

In 1955, Sam attended a reunion of First Campers, and surprisingly, he enjoyed it. In 1957, in reply to an invitation to "fall in" with the First Campers again in Ft. Worth, Sam declined, writing, "that long, tall thin man around here that wears the high hat, the striped pants and the gray whiskers put this 8th Dough-boy on a fatigue detail and watches so closely there is no chance to duck it. So please don't carry me as AWOL, merely as 'absent on TDY' [Temporary Duty]." He also praised his old friends:

> Having had considerable experience with various Mili-
> tary Units since 1916 and having expended considerable time
> and effort to encourage and assist and keep alive several
> Regimental and Division Veterans Associations, it seems
> incredible to me that the graduates of the First Officers
> Training Camp at Leon Springs have maintained their dash,
> go, and tenacity these past 41 years. That they have done so,
> and will continue to do so, until the last member meets his
> Maker, is clear evidence of the calibre of the group and the
> very hard work done by some or many.[2]

Sam was not ordered to undergo a physical examination when he arrived at Leon Springs. The only one he had received since he enlisted in the Texas Militia had been completed in June of 1916, at which time Sam was found to be in excellent health with the exception of his eyes. Why Sam went unexamined at Leon Springs is unknown; nor is it clear why his current and only physical lacked careful official scrutiny. Had such been accomplished, the military career of Sam Williams would have ended immediately. The mental and physical standards of the day were exacting, and few exceptions were made or waivers granted.

Sam did not volunteer to be again plumbed, poked, probed, thumped, and sounded. He was aware that his nearsightedness would make him ineligible and therefore end his aspirations to be commissioned. But "myopia, bilateral, correctable with glasses" would confront him again in 1919 when he applied for a commission in the Regular Army. Throughout the years that followed, Sam held doctors and dentists in high regard because they were essential to maintaining the health of a command. But he deemed his health to be his personal responsibility, and he was determined never to be physically disqualified by a junior medical officer no matter that officer's diplomas or medical credentials.

Monday, 15 May 1917, marked the first day of ninety designed to push the candidates as far as possible. Col. Stewart D. Hervey later recalled, "It was the hardest ninety days of physical and mental torture you could survive. They tried the very soul of a man."[3]

The original directives stressed that the first requisites of the instruction were to instill in the candidates thoroughness and precision in fundamentals and details. Where possible, the instruction was to be based on the realities of the war being fought in Europe. Every hour from the first was to be budgeted and efficiently expended toward producing an officer capable of performing the duties of an instructor, a manager, and a leader. It was a challenge for the more than three thousand candidates who began the course. Less than sixty percent would survive the three months of climate, Cosmoline, chiggers, and continuing uncertainty of their future.

Sam, as a member of the Eighth Company, continued to assist those less wise in martial affairs and later acknowledged that the course was not particularly difficult for him. He worked extensively as an assistant instructor because he himself had recently learned about the subjects being presented to the candidates. His training along the U.S.–Mexican border was valuable to him. Daily, he assisted or dealt directly with matters common to the qualifications of a line sergeant of 1917. He was familiar with field fortifications, field sanitation, first aid, attack and defense problems, as well as the use of explosives. But he avoided showing boredom and remained attentive when he was not assisting a principal instructor.

Throughout the officer training course, Sam exhibited a polished knowledge of the basic skills of soldiering. He was fascinated by the teaching techniques that the camp instructors used. But at the same time, he became aware of his own academic limitations, recognizing that he was ill-prepared to compete with military academy graduates and those who obtained their commissions through study at Virginia Military Institute of the Citadel. He listened to the speech of the regular officers and realized that his education was lacking and needed his personal attention. He marveled at the ease with which officers could touch on historical events in order to magnify the importance of a particular tactical exercise, and their frequent references to world military leaders, past and present, made him aware of still another personal deficiency. He mentally catalogued his educational shortcomings and resolved to correct them through self-study. To improve his literacy, he read the classics and associated with people he considered well-grounded in history, English, warfare, and geography.

More than forty years later, he told the members of the U.S. Military Academy First Classmen of his self-education: "I have long been a heavy reader and sometimes student of military campaigns and of the commanders who took part in them and their influence on history, [and] it was natural for me to wonder why certain commanders or leaders did just exactly what they did at certain times and places. This in turn led to the comparison of the actions of one to the actions of another." He cautioned the cadets, "Your study of powerful leaders and how they came to power should not be limited to persons high in our government and military circles. Become aware of your potential enemies, their country history, and their history of tactics and their philosophy in the conduct of war."[4]

Through his desire to improve, he learned about the history of the American people and their government, the principles of warfare as developed by Napoleon, and the evolution of war strategy. Throughout his years in uniform, he never traveled without a book that he could open and read for a few minutes when the occasion arose. His library grew as the years passed. Ganoes' *History of the United States Army*, Fullers' *Decisive Battles of the USA*, biographies of World War I and II leaders, military manuals, books related to China and its leaders, the *Autobiography of Benjamin Franklin*, and the *Manual for Courts-Martial 1917* were prominent in his self-improvement reading program. He frequently referred to them while collecting others.

In particular, he enjoyed reading anything that touched on the life of Benjamin Franklin. One story from Franklin's autobiography that a newly assigned unit chaplain was certain to hear from Sam involved a Presbyterian minister who served with Franklin during the French–Indian War. The minister, a Mr. Beatty, complained to Franklin that the men did not generally attend his prayers and exhortations. Franklin was aware that each man was allowed a quarter of a pint of rum a day as partial payment for his service. Franklin observed that they were punctual in assembling twice a day for their ration and suggested to the minister that he take charge of the spirits distribution. "If you were to deal it out and only just after prayers," Franklin told him, "you would have them all about you." Both Franklin and the minister were pleased with improved attendance at prayers.

Whenever Sam discussed the physical training and conditioning of soldiers, he routinely mentioned the Battle of Marathon in 490 B.C. The Persians were in defensive positions along the coast plains twenty miles north of Athens, and the Greek general, Miltiades, occupied the hills overlooking the plains and the coast.

There, he prepared for battle, giving extraordinary attention to the physical preparation and hardening of his 12,000 infantrymen by training them in the Grecian exercises of athletics and wrestling. When the trumpet sounded for action, the Greeks attacked at a full run from the hills and knolls. Lightly armed and unencumbered by heavy body shields, they bore down on the Persians, who were surprised and unprepared for engagement. The Greeks continued their advance beyond the enemy outposts, destroying unmounted cavalry and archers and dispatching the infantry with ease. The untiring Greeks lost 192 men, leaving 6,400 Persians strewn on the bloody plain of Marathon. Sam stressed that physical conditioning won the day for the Greeks.

His studies continued, and he improved his knowledge of history and warfare. But his grasp of grammar did not improve until much later. When Capt. Sam Williams attended the U.S. Army Infantry Officers Advance Course in 1930–31, he was required to write a monograph on a military subject of his choice. He wrote of his brief experience as the company commander of Company I, 359th Infantry Regiment, Ninetieth Division. It is a tiring piece to read. Misspellings, poor punctuation, and ill-selected words and verbs abound. Colloquialisms and awkward sentence structure obscure the writer's intent to tell his experiences and allow the reader to draw conclusions based on the presented information. Later, however, Sam's student writings at the Command and Staff School and the Army War College offer scant opportunity for the critic to fault his aim, accuracy, overall preparation, and writing competency. The quality of his writing had become that expected of a student attending those institutions. A 1934 United States Military Academy graduate, Col. Nathaniel Ward III, served as General Williams' chief of staff in Vietnam for two years. His daily official contact with Sam convinced him that Sam "was the finest letter, scenario, and efficiency report writer I have ever known."[5]

When a Department of State representative asked General Williams years later if he spoke French, he replied that he was not proficient in any language other than English. In this area of his educational limitation, Sam failed to follow the example of Benjamin Franklin, who, in 1733 at the age of twenty-seven, taught himself French. After becoming proficient in it, Franklin continued his efforts and mastered Italian and conversational Spanish. Yet Sam's inability to speak foreign languages was never a handicap in his dealing directly with civilian and military leaders of Korea, Germany, Turkey, Japan, Greece, and Vietnam. His demeanor, carriage, and charisma carried him beyond spoken communication. His knowledge of the matter and his skill in directing people to the heart of the subject led observers to conclude that he was familiar with the language. One of his interpreters in Saigon said it was uncanny how General Williams understood Vietnamese officials; before they had completed their response to his query, he was using their answer to form another question. The interpreter could never understand it and thought that perhaps General Williams was proficient in the language.[6] Obviously, the interpreter was unaware of the preparations Sam made before any serious discussion.

On 19 July 1917, along with the other First Campers, Sam was directed to complete a questionnaire titled "Form For Individual Record of Candidate." It contained ten general questions, including "give the exact date and place of your birth." Sam's answer in his handwriting was "July 25, 1896. Denton Texas," even though he was actually born 25 August 1897. He felt he had reason for this deception, for if the truth of his age became known, he would be ineligible for a commission. The federal regulations of the day required that officer candidates be twenty-one years old at the time of commissioning, and Sam would not attain his majority until 1918.

Many years later, for a reason known only to himself, Lt. Gen. Williams, then stationed in South Vietnam, requested a correction of official documents that referred to his date of birth. In a letter to the Department of the Army dated 15 April 1957, he asked that, "[my] records be changed to reflect my correct date of birth as shown on the attached birth certificate."

The letter, when received by the adjutant general, caused much speculation and many questions throughout the Pentagon hierarchy. Conjecture abounded as to Sam's health, possible difficulties with the South Vietnamese, and family and financial problems. Those who knew he was to retire in 1958 saw it as a ploy to gain another year of power and status. Those of lesser rank saw it as a blunder of such proportion that it gave occasion to discipline a commissioned remnant of World War I. The administrative turmoil generated by Sam's letter was felt in the office of the chief of staff. The secretary of the army, Wilbur Brucker, was uneasy too, for he felt it could lead to political embarrassment for the Eisenhower administration. Brucker ordered a thorough investigation of Sam's records as related to his age, denying a subordinate's recommendation that General Williams be returned to the Pentagon to face a formal inquiry.

A completed investigation was soon forwarded to General Taylor and to Brucker. Both agreed with the adjutant general's recommendation that Sam's request for the correction of his birth date in his official records be approved. Brucker was influenced by the investigation's discovery that Sam had, in 1951, made a similar request that had gone unanswered.

The approval to correct the records advanced Sam's mandatory retirement date to 31 August 1959.

Sam's contribution to the investigation was a one-page letter in which he admitted that he always knew his birth date was 25 August 1897. He explained how his first sergeant and the company clerk had changed his birthday when they realized that Sam would not be twenty-one years old when the Officers Training Course ended in August of 1917. In this official letter, Sam may have continued the age deception. The matter would be simplified if it could be demonstrated that Line Sergeant Williams was in fact the company clerk. Such evidence remains to be discovered. Still, it must be concluded that Sam participated in the age falsification on the officer school application.

In certain U.S. military forces, such an act would be considered an act of patriotism.

One year, three months, and five days after enlisting, Sam took the oath of office as a second lieutenant, infantry section, Officers Reserve Corps. Standing in the shade of a barracks at Leon Springs, Texas, he changed the blue braid on his campaign hat to the gold worn by officers. His bright golden bars of commissioned authority were correctly placed on his new service uniform.

No drums rolled or trumpets sounded as he departed one dusty Texas camp for another. His order directed him to report to the Ninetieth Division, Camp Travis, Texas.

(Next page) 1st Lt. Samuel T. Williams, Versig, Germany, 1919.

Chapter 4 ☆ ☆ ☆ *France 1918*

Lieutenant Williams returned to Denton by train via San Antonio, Austin, Waco, and Dallas for a two-week sojourn with his family and friends. Met by his family at the station on Railroad Avenue, he received a Texas welcome. Obviously, they were immensely proud of him and his military accomplishments. To his sisters especially, he was a dashing officer who carried with ease and assuredness his 170 pounds on his nearly six feet of muscular frame.

For the most part, Sam used his time at home to renew friendships with former classmates. Unexpectedly, he met Lt. Homer L. Fry, who had also just been commissioned at Leon Springs. Sam invited Fry to his home where they discussed at length the recent "battle" that they both had won. Soon after his return Sam spent an afternoon with Major Owsley in his office on Courthouse Square. They discussed the war and reviewed the current military situation in Europe. Owsley suggested that Sam should get a Regular Army commission—the first time anyone had mentioned to Sam that he might consider the army as a career. Both recognized that Sam's lack of a college education would be an unfavorable factor, and the present time and circumstances denied Sam the opportunity to work for a college degree. But he was secretly enthusiastic that Owsley considered him material for the regular establishment. At the moment, he wanted to become the best platoon leader in whatever regiment to which he was assigned.

When Sam reported to the Ninetieth Division headquarters at Camp Travis, 29 August 1917, he asked to be assigned to a regiment as a rifle platoon leader. Within hours he was saluting Capt. C.D. Jones of Company I, 359th Infantry. Sam was pleased because his assignment was essential to the unit needs, and he was eager to demonstrate the skills and instructional techniques he had learned as a First Camper.

With the arrival in September of draftees, Sam went to work with dedication and energy. He was a sincere young officer who recognized his responsibility to prepare the recruits for trench warfare. The training was strenuous, but most of the members of Sam's platoon were apt and willing to learn. Sam's life was busy, with instructional or range duties by day and attendance at officer's schools at night. His load of training hours was heavy because practically all of the division's noncommissioned officers had to be raised from the ranks. Wholesale transfers of junior officers placed a heavier burden on those who remained. The personnel turbulence brought the combat potential of the division to zero. For the first time while wearing a uniform, Sam became discouraged. He could see the war in Europe drawing to a close and feared that he would not be a member of the victorious force, which he was certain would be the nations of the Allied camp.

Several officers of the French army were serving with the Ninetieth Division at Camp Travis. Their task was to assist with training and give American officers advice about weapons and tactical techniques being used against the Germans. Sam made friends with one—Lt. Paul Selliers—and as time permitted, they discussed the war. Sam was interested in trench warfare, the handling of casualties, and the maintenance of morale under the most harrowing of stalemate fighting.

Most trenches were hastily dug—hardly knee deep ruts— and offered little protection from machine gun fire, mortars, or fast-firing field guns. Trench life improved as stalemates along the front continued. Eventually, some frontline defensive works, with communicating lateral passages and elaborate overhead cover, offered trench occupants a degree of protection. Yet, according to Selliers, the life of the occupying soldiers was a miserable, disgusting test of survival. Freezing rains and winds magnified the suffering of the forward infantrymen; rain flooded the ditches and trenches. Men were filthy, uniforms stank, and sanitation and waste removal were primitive. With characteristic French disdain, Selliers claimed that captured German trenches were the worst.

Of the weapons being used, the machine gun found favor with both forces because of its lethality, range, and comparatively inexpensive cost. Selliers' words about the use of high-angle mortars and long-range indirect fire pieces impressed Sam because he knew that his division had two dozen 155-millimeter howitzers and nearly fifty seventy-five-millimeter guns, but his knowledge of their use was abysmal.

At about this time in early 1918, a basic artillery course for infantry officers was scheduled. The schooling, to be conducted at Fort Sill, Oklahoma, was designed to teach to junior infantry officers the fundamentals of artillery employment and fire adjustment. Sam applied for the course immediately because he saw it as a vehicle to France and the war. His application was accepted but then revoked. Wiser heads at division headquarters knew that the current train loads of incoming trainees were going to remain with the division.

By April of 1918, the Ninetieth was brought to full strength. Feverish training followed, and not a single hour of daylight was lost. The troops were marched to the firing ranges in darkness and returned to their quarters well after sunset. After a day of instruction, they were still not free to do anything other than prepare for movement to the trenches of France. Holidays were abandoned, and Saturday training continued late into the night. Sunday also was just another training day, although time was given to those who asked a chance to attend religious services. Sam noted a considerable increase in the number of his soldiers who responded to the bugler's "Church Call."

Years later, when training a post–World War II regiment, Colonel Samuel T. Williams reminded his principal subordinates of the admonition of Civil War general Joe Hooker: "No one will consider the day as ended until the duties it brings have been discharged."

The Ninetieth Division began its journey to the trenches in France, 5 June 1918.

A slightly wounded and gassed Lt. Sam Williams took command of Company I of the 359th on the dreary morning of 16 September 1918. He was pleased but not surprised to become a commander, for he was aware that the company grade officers of the Third Battalion had experienced heavy losses during the St. Mihiel attack that had begun at first light, 12 September. Having just been promoted to first lieutenant, Sam assumed command with confidence and a certainty that this company "wasn't going to be the only one I own."[1] He accurately saw his long-range future and his role as a company commander because he would practice the art of command at the company level for 108 months, or nine years. Years later he remarked, "I did not make colonel by being a staff officer or a student. I learned to be a colonel and a commander when I was signing company morning reports in Camp Lewis, Washington; Schofield Barracks, Hawaii; and Fort Benning, Georgia."[2]

Sam's remarks about preparing to be a senior commander while serving as a small unit commander ring true. As a company commander, he faced to a lesser degree the same challenges of command that are commonplace to a regimental or division commander. A company captain was expected to routinely solve problems generated by soldiers, and at the lowest administrative level, the company commander was expected to identify and prevent them when possible. Personnel matters, training, the use and protection of government property, discipline, law and order, esprit de corps, and company harmony are the elements of daily soldiering that escalate for colonels and generals. The art of command is learned by experience, just as First Lieutenant Williams instinctively knew as he surveyed his first command.

Company I of the 359th was, he found, tired, wet, cootie-plagued, underfed, and understaffed. Sam was the only officer in the company, the others having been seriously wounded and evacuated to hospitals located south of the St. Mihiel battleground. Fifty soldiers, including some key noncommissioned officers, had fallen since August, for the Germans had harassed the company with sporadic gassing and punishing artillery fire. But the soldiers, tested by their first battle, had conducted themselves well. Sam was proud of them and told them so. He was also pleased with himself because he was in command of his physical emotions under fire. Although his heart pounded, his cool head prevented any body gestures or movements that suggested fear. Some of his fellow officers admired his personal control in the midst of falling artillery fire and the stunning slap of machine gun bullets. Others felt it was unnecessary "showboating" that moved him forward. Whatever the catalyst, Sam did move, and always in the direction that pointed to the accomplishment of his mission.

Sam's first personnel action as the company commander was to relieve the company first sergeant. "I had watched him under fire, and he was detrimental to the fighting guts of the company," Sam said. "When I kicked his yellow ass off my terrain, I thought I would hear about it, for he was admired at regimental headquarters. He was impressive on the parade ground but worthless on the battlefield."[3] Sam chose Sgt. Paul D. Hill of Fulbright, Texas, to be his acting company top-kick. He relied on Sergeant Hill for advice and assistance, particularly after he was wounded slightly on 13 September 1918. As a member of the leading attack battalion, Sam was hit by machine gun fire shortly after leaving his platoon trench. His wound, a ragged puncture located on his right calf just above the Achilles tendon, caused pain and crippled his agility as he moved through barbed wire entanglements. At the head of his platoon, he found a heavy German walking stick under a dead German officer. Sam picked it up and used it to stabilize his crippled gait.

But the now limping company commander never swerved from his duty and dedication to his troops. He talked to every noncommissioned soldier as time permitted—his unit was under fire day and night. Sam wrote later that "morale was not of the best and could possibly be considered to be below average."[4] He directed a number of measures to be taken immediately that would, to a degree, change the physical discomforts the company endured. The mess sergeant was ordered to get and keep the company fed "before you ever go to sleep." The supply sergeant, who had passed Sam's muster, was told to locate and return to the soldiers their bed rolls, which had been left in a quartermaster dump before the recent offensive. Sam also ordered an extra amount of all types of ammunition to be on hand and distributed to every rifleman as needed.

Sam organized the company into three platoons of full-strength units. He transferred inefficient and lazy noncommissioned officers and reduced others he felt were "ribbon clerks." He removed from the jurisdiction of a favored few the stocks of alcoholic beverages captured in the move forward and he ordered their equal and controlled distribution to all ranks. First Sergeant Hill was directed to prepare recommendations for awards for those men known to have contributed significantly to the recent combat success of the company. He agitated the staff at battalion to expedite the delivery of his soldiers' mail. He also paid attention to the distribution of company-prepared food in order to assure that each soldier had an equal measure and that it was available to all—even visitors. Recognizing that although trenches would never provide the comforts of an army barracks, Sam improved what they had by installing duck boards, correcting drainage, and providing for a heavy, overhead cover.

In these days of his first command, Sam leaned on his soldiers to improve. Most of them were young, with fewer than five months in uniform. He demanded that they maintain their weapons daily so that they fired without fail. As he moved through his frontline positions, he checked the guns by firing them toward German lines. Sam was also concerned about field sanitation. The area captured from the Germans was a quagmire of stinking, dead animals, manure, exposed human feces, and rat droppings. His immediate orders called for cleaning, burying, and burning all matter that could possibly be damaging to the health of his soldiers. He directed the mess sergeant to provide large pots of boiling water to eradicate "cooties" from the men's clothing.

His dealings with the battalion supply officer, Lt. Walter Grothaus, helped to improve the unit spirit. Grothaus had also been a First Camper in the Eighth Company, and Sam found his good friend cooperative when the frontline troops were rotated. It was the practice at the time to rotate the frontline platoons because the drudgery of continuous trench occupation soon made the strongest soldiers inefficient. Sam, as the company commander, instituted the rotation system when he was confident that it could be completed with minimum disruption. Grothaus was a great help, and years later, Lieutenant General Williams said with affection of Grothaus: "He was waiting every time I brought an outfit out of the front line. He would give my mess sergeant additional rations and had much hot food prepared for immediate eating. He would have a wagon load of such things as dry clothing, raincoats, automatic rifle magazine clips, stationery, chocolate, soap, and towels. He was a wonderful officer, who knew about soldier morale. I never questioned him as to where the captured pistols, flags, bottles of cognac, or wine went."[5]

Sam bristled when he remembered a similar World War II situation: "I told a '4' to assist a frontline forward unit by replenishing the needs of the unit for it was obvious they required toothpaste, cigarettes, rations, grenades, and ammunition. This '4' sent an assistant to the beleaguered battalion commander asking him to send back a signed requisition as to his needs. A helluva clown that '4' was."[6]

In late September of 1918, Sam made his first serious mistake as company commander. A new officer, well-schooled in matters of infantry but having no battle experience, was assigned to Company I. Sam oriented him and conducted a frontline walk, introducing him to the terrain in front of the company. He then ordered the young man to conduct a night patrol to the front with a mission of capturing a German. The company patrol, under the leadership of the novice lieutenant, left at dusk. Within an hour after its departure, Sam heard grenade explosions coming from the area he knew was on the patrol's route. Soon, he alerted his entire company because it sounded as if the Germans were advancing; however, it was Company I's patrol returning on the run, and as Sam said, "their wind was up." When he investigated what had caused the patrol's early and unexpected return, Sam uncovered this story: The company reached the first danger point and had been challenged by a German outpost. The new officer gave an order to "throw grenades," and the company did so. But then the inexperienced officer commanded, "To the rear, on the double." The soldiers hurriedly returned to the company location, leaving the Germans as confused as they were. Sam later said of the failed patrol, "It was a serious mistake for me to send a new officer on patrol on his first day on the front line. This was especially true for he did not know the soldiers nor did they know him. Thankfully, no lives were lost or wounds suffered. I never made a similar mistake again."[7]

During this first command, Sam also confronted an officer superior to him in rank and position. On one of the few occasions he visited his immediate headquarters, he had several points he wanted to discuss with the battalion commander, Maj. Tom Collins. Collins at the moment was directing the reinforcement of his personal bunker and seemingly had little time to talk to his company commander. Collins asked Sam if he felt the sand-bagged bunker could withstand a direct German artillery hit. The question annoyed Sam, who sarcastically replied, "It is far safer in the battalion rear area in a major's bunker than it is at the front exposed to all types of fire."[8]

This unwitnessed altercation continued to be a source of irritation to Sam; he persisted in finding fault with every order coming from Collins' command post. Nor did Collins fail to notice Sam's sarcasm. Within hours after he had expressed his caustic remarks, Sam was directed to report to Major Collins. Expecting to be relieved of his command now that it had another officer, Sam was mildly surprised when he received orders to send out a platoon-sized patrol during the night that was to penetrate enemy lines and was to return with prisoners. He was issued sixteen shot guns and four boxes of ammunition for patrol use.

Sam prepared a patrol to carry out his orders and decided to lead it himself. Contrary to his orders to use a platoon, Sam selected twenty-five of the company's finest soldiers. He armed sixteen of them with shot guns and gave instructions on how to fire them and under what conditions they were to be used against the "Boche." (During World War II, General Williams occasionally referred to the German soldiers as "Boche," to the amusement of anyone overhearing him.) He took the entire patrol to a high elevation overlooking the area that they were to penetrate and briefed them on the route he intended to follow.

After dark, he moved his patrol forward over rough terrain. The stars came out, and visibility improved. The patrol was challenged by someone speaking German from a patch of woods to its front, but they still could not make out the speaker. A member of the patrol spoke German, and Sam used him to convince the Germans that the patrol was a German raiding party heading for the American lines. He then ordered the patrol to attack the woods from which the voice came, cautioning them to avoid shooting patrol members and urging them to take prisoners. They advanced to the woods, killing one German and wounding another en route. Sam moved forward to a small building near the edge of the woods. The door of the shed was ajar. He stood with his back to the door, observing his patrol and planning on its next movement. Suddenly, he felt the door move, and from the shack stepped a German officer with his back to Sam. Sam dropped the man with the end of the walking stick he had taken from the dead German officer at the beginning of the St. Mihiel offensive. He then relieved the officer of his pistol and directed a patrol member to return to the American lines with the stunned prisoner. The prisoner was told to move, but he collapsed to the ground. The wary patrol member bayoneted the prisoner instantly, and Sam, in order to save the prisoner's life, knocked the guard down with the same cane that had just felled the German officer. He once again instructed the patrol member to deliver the man alive to the American lines. Sam said that after his instruction, the soldier was more afraid of his company commander than of the Germans.

The patrol was reassembled with difficulty, for the successes that the members had achieved made them eager to engage the entire German Army. It was time, however, to begin moving to friendly lines. Sam led them, with a total of three captured Germans closely watched by every patrol member. Sam later said that he was not surprised when, after moving a few yards, he discovered the captured German officer and his patrol guard sharing the same shell crater. They were both added to the spirited patrol, which passed without further interruption through friendly lines to the 360th Infantry Regiment sector.

Sam took the entire group and the prisoners to his battalion headquarters where he was relieved of the Germans, and the patrol was told to return to Company I. Sam was directed to report to his regimental commander, Col. E.K. Sterling. Sterling congratulated Sam profusely. The members of the patrol were, unfortunately, not present to hear Colonel Sterling's commendatory remarks.

Lieutenant Sam T. Williams was a proud company commander when he returned to Company I. Assembling the patrol members and as many other company soldiers as he could gather, he told the group of Colonel Sterling's complimentary words. Sam was proud and beamed with joy; nonetheless, he remained the commander and ordered the shot guns to be cleaned, as well as the other weapons the patrol had carried. The entire company enjoyed extra food, with a double portion of wine for those who wanted it.

Just after the noon meal, Sam was again ordered to report to Major Collins without delay. Before Sam's salute was completed, Collins was charging him with dereliction of duty, which could be properly punished by relief, arrest in quarters, and court-martial. Sam interrupted Collins to say, "I would welcome a period of rest in the safety of the Major's bunker, and what are you accusing me of, Sir?" Collins told him that during the patrol, Sam had permitted his soldiers to steal a watch, a gold ring, and twenty German paper marks from the captured prisoners.

Sam returned to his company, thinking what a cruel world it was.

Acting First Sergeant Hill listened as his company commander explained Major Collins' threats. Hill excused himself when Sam finished his story but returned within twenty minutes. He told Sam that he could cover stolen deutsche marks in any amount. Hill then emptied a paper bag filled with watches and gold rings, asking Sam as he did so, "Sir, which of these rings and watches are the ones reported to have been stolen?" Collins' threats never materialized, nor was Sam ever questioned about the pistol he appropriated from the captured German officer.

Sam commanded his first company for more than thirty days before he relinquished it to a newly arrived captain. He left it reluctantly for he had discovered a deep satisfaction in caring for his soldiers and in serving with them as they faced danger and hardship. He responded to their allegiance with a loyalty and personal support that extended to the lowest ranking private in the company.

After leaving Company I, Sam was posted to battalion headquarters as a scout officer because his reputation had spread following his successful raid and patrol into the enemy lines during the night. The intelligence officer, Lt. Herbert G. Terry, another Eighth Company First Camper at Leon Springs, was aware of Sam's hostility toward Major Collins and managed to keep them separated. Collins, for his part, avoided further confrontation. As scout officer, Sam prepared written estimates and local terrain studies and conducted some limited reconnaissance activities.

He was rested and pleased when ordered to take command once again of his old company. His challenge when he returned was to prepare the company for movement with the other units of the 359th to a new battle sector above the Meuse River line. The move, complete by mid-October, was made by truck without incident and was a welcome respite from the frontline uncertainties of deadly artillery and machine gun fire.

The 359th was placed in division reserve at its new location. It was subjected to heavy harassing fire that took a toll on officers and men. A beloved chaplain, Capt. Charles D. Priest, was killed as he was officiating at a burial service of both American and German troops.

The heaviest fighting that the Third Battalion faced in their new sector occurred 2 November 1918. The Germans had skillfully positioned machine guns to cover the principal routes of advance. Also, the long-range observed artillery fire was devastating to the forward elements. Company I was placed in support of Company M and a company from the Second Battalion. When the regimental objective was taken, Sam's company helped defeat a heavy counterattack delivered by a fresh German force. Another counterattack was unsuccessful, but the Germans gave little evidence of withdrawing from the area. The two-day regimental attack in which Sam's company had participated was a successful effort, yielding many prisoners, field guns, and artillery pieces, plus huge stocks of abandoned supplies.

Records do not reflect any extraordinary contributions to the endeavor by Company I during the Meuse–Argonne campaign. But, wrote Sam in 1930, "It was as good as any company in the regiment and was so considered. It performed excellent work throughout the war."[9]

On November 8th, the division ordered the 180th Brigade and its two regiments—the 359th and 360th—to become division reserves. Then within hours, the brigade received another order to cross the Meuse in its sector beginning November 9th. During the night, the 359th crossed the river and seized the heights on the opposite shore.

The fighting on the day preceding the armistice was severe and costly, and one of the wounded officers was Lieutenant Samuel T. Williams, commander of Company I, 359th Infantry Regiment. A German artillery round exploded to his immediate rear as he moved with his leading platoon toward a key hilltop in his area. The jagged fragments were deeply embedded in his back, along with the debris of his clothing. He was hit at 2:30 P.M., 10 November 1918.

World War I ended the next morning.

Sam was in pain as he was carried to the 359th medical station on a stretcher. There, he was given emergency treatment and evacuated to the AEF Mobile Hospital, where he was heavily sedated and transferred to Army Field Hospital-156. After his physical condition stabilized, he was transported to Army Hospital-30, where he remained until 20 January 1919.

Two weeks before Christmas of 1918, Sam's mother was notified of his serious wound. Less than two weeks earlier, she had been advised of the gunshot wound to his right leg. The notification of December 12th caused her to be depressed, and one grandson recalled that "Grandma Williams cried a lot, even through the holidays."[10]

Lt. Gen. Samuel T. Williams carried to his grave a "metal foreign body, 5 x 4 mm." It was embedded in his left chest, one of the few souvenirs of World War I that he retained during the years of his long military service and retirement.

Seventy-one days after medics carried him to the rear, Sam returned once again to the Ninetieth Division, hoping to take command of his favorite rifle company then located in Kinheim, Germany.

(Above) Lt. Col. Samuel T. Williams, Camp Swift, Texas, 1942; Ninety-fifth Infantry Division G4.

(Next page) Jewell Spear became Mrs. Samuel T. Williams in 1921.

Chapter 5 ☆ ☆ ☆ *The Old Army*

As Lieutenant Williams was recuperating in Clermont-Ferrand, France, the Ninetieth Division went to Germany to serve as part of the Army of Occupation. The area assigned to the division was along a stretch of the Moselle River, a region of dramatic landscapes laced with terraced vineyards. In World War II, General Patton's Third Army located four of its divisions in the area from the Rhine River north to Luxembourg, which was the trace of the 1918 Army of Occupation responsibility.

While Sam was hospitalized, he pondered his future and came to realize that a military career offered him the type of activity and opportunity he sought. He had no firm wish to return to Denton because it held no challenge for him with its farms and related agricultural pursuits. His hours of meditation brushed away notions of the surgical gown, the business suit of commerce, or the robes of a judge. Nor did he want to spend his years on a college campus. Somehow, a cap and gown was unappealing to him after witnessing the heroism and sacrifices of ordinary, unlettered soldiers. He reflected that his character meshed with the traditional restrictions of a military vocation and that he was not opposed to the discipline of the army and its inherent demands for personal sacrifice. His spirit marched to the drummer's beat of the obligations of citizenship and allegiance to the nation. His three years of service had influenced him because he had discovered personal satisfaction in leading men, individually and collectively. He knew he could bridge the demands placed on a junior army officer for he had demonstrated that he could instruct, shelter, feed, arouse loyalty, and inspire courage and self-reliance in soldiers. Most importantly, he had proved to himself and others that he was a courageous leader in battle.

So while he was a patient in Army Hospital-30, Sam decided to become a Regular Army officer. He wasted no time and questioned his doctors about his physical condition; they assured him he would recover fully, with only a few scars remaining. Aware of his nearsightedness, he arranged for a thorough study by the staff ophthalmologist, who found no improvement in his faulty vision.

Sam discussed his vision defect with several Regular Army officers who also were patients. Their advice was to apply for a regular commission, emphasizing his experience as a successful platoon leader and company commander in two campaigns where he experienced no difficulty because of a minor sight defect.

When he returned to the Ninetieth in February of 1919, Sam expected to be given, once again, his company, but to his disappointment, he was assigned as adjutant to the Second Battalion—his first staff job. Nonetheless, he managed to find the adjutant position educational, and he enjoyed being privy to information heretofore unavailable to him. He developed an appreciation for the functions of a staff and the key role it played in the support of a commander and the lower command elements.

Maj. William R. Brown commanded his battalion in a calm, even-handed manner, quite unlike the timid, nervous

Major Collins of the Third Battalion. Brown was patient with his inexperienced adjutant, whom he found to be careless in matters calling for meticulous attention to detail, especially in administrative actions dealing with personnel. Sam accepted the counseling, but a few years later in a similar assignment, he was found to demonstrate less than an ordinary proficiency in giving priority attention to administrative matters.

In early March of 1919, Sam forwarded to division headquarters an "Application for Examination for Appointment/Regular Army." Included in the completed application was a recommendation dated 17 December 1918 from Colonel E.K. Sterling of the 359th, whom knew Sam well. Sterling favored approval, including the comment, "Lieutenant Williams has the qualities requisite to the grade of First Lieutenant Infantry, Regular Army. He is intelligent, active, and of good character. He has the necessary force and energy for the position sought."

The applicant was soon scheduled for an examination. The Board of Examiners consisted of five senior officers, two of whom were medical consultants. When the board convened, Col. H.B. Farrar, the board president, stressed to Sam that the board before which he was appearing was not the final examining board. Sam said he understood. Then Sam was asked if he objected to a physical examination by the two medical officers. Sam did not object, so he proceeded to an examining room with the two consultants. When the physical was completed, the three returned to the hearing and the board reconvened. The senior medical officer reported that they found, after a detailed examination, that the applicant was physically unfit for duty as a Regular Army officer because of vision impairment. The board members therefore voted that Sam be disqualified for service as a member of the Regular Army.

The board's decision was a heavy blow to Sam and shattered his hopes. He was hurt and burdened emotionally with embarrassment and disappointment. Nonetheless, he vowed to try again, and if he were unsuccessful a second time, he would reevaluate his ambition.

Events prevented Sam from becoming despondent or

sullen. Disillusioned as he was at the time, he recovered quickly when told he was to return to command Company I of the 359th.

His soldiers, he discovered, were active and busy in a variety of programs, including participation in schools, athletics, and traveling. An announcement that division soldiers were eligible to participate in competition that could lead to entry in the forthcoming Interallied Games caught Sam's attention. He raised a volunteer platoon from his best riflemen and began training for division elimination contests in musketry firing. He appointed himself the platoon leader—a curious organizational feat, for as company commander, he commanded himself as a company platoon leader. Although they faced experienced competition, he and his volunteers were among the 209 officers and soldiers selected to represent the division at Le Mans, France, in June of 1919.

By that time, the Ninetieth was to be relocated to Camp Bowie, Texas, scheduled for demobilization. The musketry platoon along with its leader was transferred to the Thirtieth Infantry Regiment, a unit of the Third Division. Sam's last regimental commander in the 359th Infantry was Col. W.A. Cavenaugh, who wrote of him in a special Efficiency Report dated 5 May 1920: "I have known this officer for seven months, during which time he has performed all the duties incident to administration and instruction of an [infantry commander] in field and camp most satisfactorily. This officer's loyalty to his superior officers and devotion to duty is exemplary." Cavenaugh elsewhere in the report wrote that Sam was above average in physical endurance, forcefulness, and military bearing. He further remarked that Sam was an excellent young officer, especially in combat and when in charge of scouts.

Sam continued training with the platoon, preparing for the matches in Le Mans during the first phase of the games. But the musketry efforts of Sam and his platoon went without recognition or applause when the records of the games were completed and final scores computed.

The Third Division returned to the United States for duty in Camp Pike, Arkansas. Sam arrived in New York 23 August

1919 and continued his journey west to Camp Pike, reporting for duty on August 27th.

Assigned to Company I, Thirtieth Infantry, Sam served as a platoon leader and was a part-time instructor in a school for the unit's noncommissioned officers. None of the duty assignments he held during this time reflect those that would normally be given an ambitious lieutenant: he was a regimental police officer, he was in charge of company administration, he served as an instructor of minor tactics, and he performed the duties of range safety officer. His performance appears to have been lackadaisical for his efficiency reports were below average in some instances.

Then, quite unexpectedly, he received a letter from the War Department telling him that his services as a first lieutenant, Officers Reserve Corps, would no longer be required as of 31 October 1919; as of that date he would be discharged from the service for the convenience of the government. Sam was greatly disturbed. At first, he was confident that the information was an administrative error, but this thought was dispelled after a hurried visit to the division adjutant general, who confirmed the notice and offered to assist him in his scheduled departure. Sam continued to be bewildered and asked to see the regimental commander.

When Sam reported to Colonel M.A. Elliot, he met a sympathetic listener who gave the young officer his full attention. Elliot's immediate observation was that Sam was a confused, bitter lieutenant whose sense of personal esteem and commitment to the army had been shattered. The two of them discussed the edict, with Elliot searching Sam's background to determine if some event of the past had formed the basis for the dismissal. Sam assured him that the only difficulty he had had in his career was with Major Collins, and that had not generated an adverse efficiency report. Sam, in turn, believed he was the victim of misidentification, for there was another Williams of the same rank in the Third Division who wanted to return to civilian life. Colonel Elliot by this time had quieted his subordinate and promised to investigate the matter.

Sam, still glum, called his older brother Ed in Fort Worth. He didn't seek relief from Ed and apparently just wanted to talk about the situation with a family member. He mentioned his suspicion that he was being confused with another officer named Williams.

Ed Williams was not one to sit on a problem when it involved a member of his family, so he visited a long-time friend, Mr. Sam Pattie, with whom he discussed his brother's telephone call. Mr. Pattie knew Sam would want a quick solution and said to Ed, "If you have no objections, I'll call Congressman Sam Rayburn in Washington to see if he can get the army to keep your brother Sam."

Congressman Rayburn listened to the story of Sam's plight as told by his caller from Grayson County, Texas. When Mr. Pattie finished, Rayburn dialed the War Department and asked for General Harris, the adjutant general. After his conversation with Rayburn, General Harris said he would look into the matter and return the congressman's call soon. Rayburn was satisfied and notified Mr. Pattie that Sam could expect to remain on active duty for as long as the World War emergency existed.

Despite the influence of Adjutant General Harris and Congressman Rayburn, First Lieutenant Williams nonetheless was greeted on the morning of 31 October 1919 as "Mister" Williams. For him, the war emergency had ended.

As he was being discharged, Sam filed an application seeking immediate recommission and subsequent duty with troops, referring to himself as "the late" First Lieutenant Williams. He returned to Denton and, after lengthy consideration, sent Congressman Rayburn a copy of his application with an explanatory letter.

On the day he received Sam's letter, Congressman Rayburn paid a call to General Harris in his War Department office. It was a short visit. The following day, November 14th, a letter was delivered from the agitated congressman to the adjutant general of the War Department:

Dear General Harris:

I desire to call your attention to the personal call made to your office today at which time I left with you papers in the case of Lt. Sam T. Williams, who is anxious to be recommissioned in the U.S. Army.

You will recall that Lt. Williams' name was at first on the list of those officers to be retained in the service after October 31, 1919, but was taken off the list a short time before that date. This, of course, placed me in an embarrassing position, as I had been assured by you by letter and telephone that Lt. Williams should be kept in the service.

In accordance with your suggestion and your promise to look after the matter personally, I have advised Lt. Williams to submit an application to the Adjutant General for reappointment and told him that I thought he would have a good chance to be reappointed. He has been strongly recommended. In view of the fact that his name was removed from the list at the very last moment, I trust you will be able to give him the first opening that occurs.

Thanking you in advance, I am
Sincerely yours,
Sam Rayburn

Mr. Sam T. Williams, formerly an officer of the U.S. National Army, was overwhelmed when he received a telegram on November 18th from the War Department ordering him to report without delay to Camp Pike for duty. General Harris wasted no time in responding to Rayburn's visit and dispatched a letter to Sam that he received six days after Congressman Rayburn's call to General Harris.

The new Lieutenant Williams was satisfied. He acknowledged the influence his congressman had used for him and dutifully wrote him a letter of sincere gratitude. Characteristically, Sam resolved to try to gain a regular commission when he felt the time and army circumstances were favorable. Until that time, he was happy to be a member of the Officer Reserve Corps and on duty to serve for an unspecified time.

Sam's primary duty on his return to active duty was recruiting as a member of an itinerant team of officers that traveled areas of eastern Oklahoma, western Mississippi, and southern Missouri, as well as the entire state of Arkansas. Colonel W.S. McBroom, the officer-in-charge, found Sam to be of average ability but indicated in an Efficiency Report dated 31 December 1920 that he would no doubt have "greater value as an officer of the line." Whatever Sam's immediate worth as an army recruiter, he managed to capture the heart of a young lady who would later swear allegiance to him and live with him as his wife for nearly sixty-three years.

The effervescent Jewell Spear was twenty-two years old and first attracted Sam's attention when she attended a dance at the Camp Pike Officer Club. Even though she was another officer's date, Sam never let her out of his sight. At the next dance, she was Sam's guest. For the eighteen months before their marriage, they were inseparable.

Sam's deepening relationship with Jewell probably helped kindle the desire for greater security than he found in the Officers Reserve Corps. He soon became convinced that it was a good time to again apply for a commission in the Regular Army. His recent experience of being discharged without warning reminded Sam of the future uncertainties he would face as a reserve officer. He had seen other reservists, some with families, suffer unexpected, heartless hardships. Sam never wanted to cause Jewell such unwarranted anguish and pain. In his own case, the unexpected mustering out left him dubious of the compassion the military hierarchy in Washington held for its officers. His welfare and that of his future wife merited a regular commission, and he decided to try once more to secure one.

For a second time, he prepared an application for a regular appointment, which was forwarded through military channels 1 April 1920. Unlike his earlier attempt, he mailed a carbon typewritten copy of his application with a personal letter to Congressman Rayburn, who telephoned the War Department adjutant general when he received Sam's letter.

After considering all available information, the examining board recommended in its report dated 15 July 1920 that Samuel T. Williams be commissioned in the Regular Army, and

Sam accepted a Regular Army commission as a First Lieutenant with a date of rank, 1 July 1920. The board noted Sam's "fairly high above-average score on the mental examination," and, curiously, made no mention in Sam's sight impairment, which had cost him so dearly in his past aspirations.

Only fifteen days later, Lieutenant Williams, who by this time was inured to the strange workings of the War Department, was promoted to captain, Regular Army—"an unusually fast rise in rank," according to Sam himself.[1] This quick promotion was due to the National Defense Act of 1920, which provided for a substantial increase in the army's strength. To fill the vacancies in the proper grades and numbers, the army selected those men who had served from the first day of World War I through the date of the act, 20 June 1920. Coincidence or fate favored Sam; he was eligible and quickly accepted his new-found rank when it was tendered in mid-July of 1920.

Now Sam's future looked promising and full of opportunity. He saw Jewell as his bride and companion; he wanted her to share his army life, which he was confident would be successful now that he was a regular. The unexpected rank of captain with its monthly pay of $220 strengthened his resolve to ask Jewell to marry him a few months later.

Jewell's brothers, Charles and Eugene, were excited participants in Sam and Jewell's marriage. Charles recalled the ceremony, which was held in the parlor of the Spear home:

> At the time of the wedding, I was sixteen. On the 21st of September 1921, I came home from school to find that Mother had our dining room table set up in a beautiful fashion. I asked her, "What is going on?" She told me it was a surprise and that I would find out at six o'clock. At that hour, Captain Williams and another officer arrived at our home by taxi. We had a delicious supper, but Gene and I didn't get to talk much. When we were finished eating, we and all the dinner guests moved to the parlor where Jewell and Sam married. The two of them left Little Rock by train that evening for Camp Lewis, Washington.[2]

The new location of the Thirtieth Infantry and its parent unit, the Third Division, was the northwest station. Sam's principal task there was adjutant of Special Troops, a loose organizational gathering represented by units of the basic service branches. Besides the routine task as adjutant, he filled several secondary positions as assistant provost marshal, personnel officer, and disbursing officer. Undoubtedly, the provost marshal's task came about because of Sam's rugged physical appearance and force of personality, each of which was frequently cited by rating officers as commendable.

Sam was again surprised by the Congress of 1922, which reduced the army's strength and slashed its monetary support. Once again, a letter from the War Department caused anguish and torment for Sam as he read that effective November 18th, he was demoted to his Regular Army rank of first lieutenant. In the first army-wide reduction-in-force, more than 1,000 officers of all grades were eliminated, and about 800 others were reduced to Regular Army rank. Sam did not dwell on it, but he later acknowledged that he found this demotion difficult to explain to Jewell.

The efficiency reports on Lieutenant or Captain Samuel T. Williams during his first eight years of commissioned service in the U.S. Army do not suggest that he was singularly worthwhile to the army and its future. On the contrary, Sam was a sometimes careless young commissioned novice who routinely rated "average" no matter the senior making the report. Even the occasional ratings submitted by colonels who had great faith in him, and said so, found him to be on a par with others of equal rank and experience. His physique, fine appearance, force of personality, and loyalty to all were often common notations concerning his general value.

Unlike others who had experienced similar mundane duty assignments—Eisenhower, MacArthur, and Patton, for instance—Sam seemed to be without a trace of McArthur's intellectual purpose, was devoid of Patton's flamboyant drive to gain prominence through the advocacy of mobile warfare, and did not demonstrate Eisenhower's staff assignment or political competency. Rather,

Sam's early commissioned years were marked with his extraordinary drive to gain the status and security of a regular commission. From the beginning, he was idealistic, but he was also satisfied with his minor achievements. In the early years of his career, his superiors generally found Sam to be energetic, loyal, and hard-working—though tactless—and a reliable officer who would develop professionally with additional service.

His service file, however, was adequate enough for him to be chosen to attend the Company Officers Course beginning in September of 1925 at Fort Benning, Georgia. For the next nine months, Sam was an attentive student who also found time to pursue his favorite sport—polo. He did not own his own mounts but rented those horses that were fleet and agile but heavy enough to withstand the frequent shock of contact with other contestants and their ponies. Sam enjoyed polo because it allowed him to demonstrate his combativeness and gave him useful exercise following the sedentary practices of a desk-bound student. He felt that the best thing for the "insides of a man is the outsides of a horse," an expression he had probably heard at Camp Lewis.

Sam graduated from Company Officers Course 30 May 1926. Col. Frank Cocheu, assistant commandant of the Infantry School, found Lieutenant Williams to be, "a loyal and dependable officer, who would give willing and generous support regardless of his personal views in the matter."[3] Sam was pleased with the report, and he and Jewell were thrilled with the forthcoming travel to Hawaii where Sam was to serve with the Twenty-first Infantry Regiment, a unit of the Hawaiian Division.

They were equally happy on July 20th when Sam was, for a second time, promoted to captain, although ten more years would pass before Captain Williams would pin the golden leaves of a major to his uniform. The nineteen years he spent as a company grade officer was not an unusual length of time for those officers who were first commissioned during World War I and who would be on continuous active duty at the time of the attack on Pearl Harbor, 7 December 1941.

When Sam reported to Schofield Barracks in early Fall, he

was given command of a machine gun company, a post he held for two years, after which he became the regimental intelligence officer. Sam's four years with the Twenty-first Infantry helped his professional development. He often had unofficial contact with Maj. George S. Patton, who was also assigned to the Hawaiian Division. Maj. Omar N. Bradley also rated Sam for a short period of duty, finding Captain Williams "very satisfactory" for his performance during a National Guard Training Camp. Overall, Sam demonstrated a greater capacity for work then he had before, perhaps because of his recent schooling at Fort Benning. His superiors found his general efficiency to be excellent or superior but adversely leavened by his continued lack of tact.

For Jewell, and to a degree Sam, the Hawaiian tour ended too quickly when in 1930 he was directed to return to Fort Benning for further advanced studies. One of his classmates he came to know well was a German army officer named Adolf von Schell, at the time a captain in Germany's regular force. Von Schell captivated Sam, who found the man to be pleasant as well as knowledgeable about World War I. The two frequently adjourned to the officer's club, where their discussions centered on the battles of the "war to end all wars." Sam discovered that Von Schell had a keen, analytical mind and demonstrated it by writing several articles for the *Infantry Journal,* a publication produced by the Infantry School. One story Von Schell told Sam was about an incident involving nervous soldiers under fire.

On the Eastern Front, according to Von Schell, his company had moved under the cover of darkness to an exposed position preparatory to making an attack. But circumstances forced them to remain in the position during the day, and Russian artillery carried out some "searching fire missions" that came close to Von Schell's position. The fire continued, and his soldiers became increasingly nervous. Von Schell calmed them by having the company barber give him a haircut in view of his men, and possibly some Russian armed lookouts. His action quieted the fearful men.

When Sam asked, "How did you make that barber stand still?" Von Schell merely smiled.[4]

After he completed the advanced course, Sam was chosen to remain at the Infantry School as an instructor; however, he declined, explaining that it didn't appeal to him. Instead, he and Jewell traveled to Fort Hamilton, New York, where Sam commanded a machine gun company in the Eighteenth Infantry, a regiment of the First Division. Soon, Sam began to think about the continued military education he knew was necessary for his promotion to higher grades. Back at Leon Springs, he had recognized his educational limitation but had done little to correct it. Now, he decided that completing the one- or two-year course at the U.S. Army Command and General Staff School (CGSS) was critical to his future.

He was aware that CGSS facilities could accommodate a limited number of students. The competition for a school desk was fierce, and the fundamental basis for comparing potential students was the efficiency report file. Only the best officers were selected, despite rumors of the importance of political influence and acquaintanceship with a member of the selection board. Sam also knew that age was a factor in the selection process, and in 1933, using his official but incorrect birth date, he was thirty-seven years old. Sam breathed easily again when the list of attendees for the two-year course (1933–35) included his name.

Sam completed the course without gaining any particular recognition or status. In recalling those years, Sam felt particularly what an honor it was to attend the class with those who were destined for positions of the highest trust in the army and the U.S. government. He held these members of his class in awe; little did he know then that he too would become a distinguished graduate of the CGSS class of 1935 and serve with Generals Maxwell Taylor, Mathew Ridgway, Mark Clark, and Walter Smith. Of the 113 members of the class, these four would become generals, and eight others would wear the three stars of lieutenant general, including Sam Williams.

After graduation, Sam returned to Fort Benning where he once again became a company commander and later a staff officer in the Twenty-ninth Infantry Regiment. Jewell occupied her time with Girl Scouts programs, while Sam once again played polo during his leisure time. For two years Sam watched the army as it slowly changed its philosophy to the spirit of the offensive. The army was moving and expanding; the infantry was being motorized, mechanized, and modernized. Of course, the army occasionally was distracted from training and cast its attention toward floods, beach repairs, the Civilian Conservation Corps, the Works Progress Administration, and the Public Works Administration, as well as other tasks that seemed "unmilitary" and alien to the infantry organization. Whatever the distractions, Sam witnessed the founding of a new division that contained three regiments of infantry, plus a reinforced artillery most professionals considered a revolutionary change for the better.

Once again, Sam was selected to continue his professional education as a student at the Army War College. The college, located in the District of Columbia, was less demanding on Sam than the course at CGSS had been. He contributed his fair share and more to student joint efforts, and he also became known as a listener who cooperated with his fellow classmates. His class standing was high when he completed the year, and it was suggested to him that he should seek assignment with the War Department general staff. He gave thoughtful consideration to such an assignment but declined it. He later wrote about the decision: "Since neither office work or city life appealed to me, I declined to seek a staff position. Maybe such a request would have been approved and again it might not have been. At any rate, my not asking was an error in judgment careerwise as the king-makers were and are in Washington. By asking for 'duty with troops,' I once more ended up at Benning, this time as Secretary to the Infantry Board."[5]

Sam was at Fort Benning from June of 1938 through May of 1942. When Pearl Harbor was attacked in December of 1941, he quickly volunteered for any combat assignment, wherever one was open, in order to follow his desire for "duty with troops." But his request letters were all denied, including the one in which he offered to attend paratrooper school to get command of a paratroop battalion.

In August of 1940, he had been promoted to lieutenant

coloncl, and by August of 1942, Sam was a colonel. He was then given command of the 378th Infantry Regiment, a unit he was commanding in March of 1943 when he was selected for promotion to brigadier general and was transferred to the Ninetieth Motorized Division. General Williams had come full circle in a quarter of a century for he was once more a member of the Ninetieth. His duty assignment was to be the assistant division commander, and he wore his first star proudly.

Lt. Sam T. Williams who joined the Ninetieth Division in 1917 was a different cut of khaki cloth than Brig. Gen. Samuel T. Williams of the Ninetieth Division in 1943. In twenty-five years, the eagerness of the idealistic youth had been replaced with maturity and a dedication to professionalism. With the exception of high-level staff duty, General Williams' background was quite adequate for the challenges of his new position. His military schooling had included every academic course offered to those who had demonstrated potential for high command. Even though Sam's record reveals an officer who, from the beginning, was little more than average, he had a rugged strength of character and a forceful, domineering spirit. He unhesitatingly spoke his mind on all occasions when asked, and on many occasions when he should have remained quiet. He made decisions swiftly and was seldom in error. Also, in 1943 he knew how to command troops; only a successful future could be predicted in World War II for Brig. Gen. Samuel T. Williams, assistant division commander, Ninetieth Motorized Division.

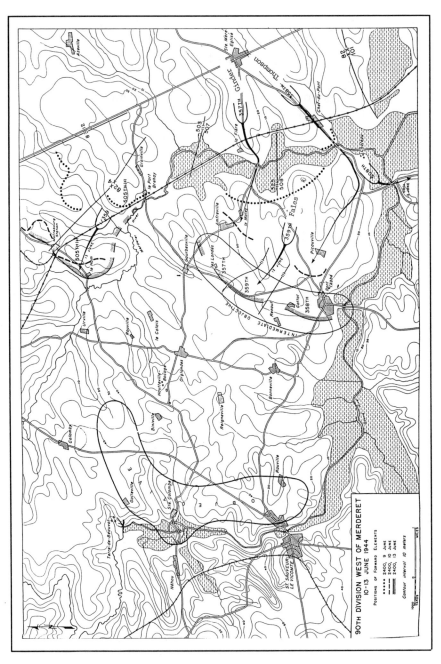

(Above) Ninetieth Division west of Merderet, 10–13 June 1944.

(Next page) Securing the Douve Line, 14–16 June 1944.

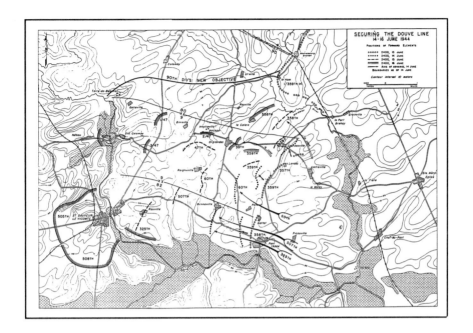

Chapter 6 ☆ ☆ ☆ Normandy, June 1944

The Allied landings on 6 June 1944 along the north shore of Normandy, France, were the culmination of two years of British and American planning. The early phases of preparation were coordinated under the chief of staff, Supreme Allied Command, Lt. Gen. Sir Frederick E. Morgan. Gen. Dwight D. Eisenhower took formal command of the integrated staff and its headquarters in February of 1944. Shortly thereafter, he appointed Gen. Bernard L. Montgomery as commander of the Twenty-first Army Group, which became the Allied operational headquarters. Montgomery began directly to forge an invasion force that would have the strength and capability to make the landings and sustain itself against the enemy, for the German High Command controlled fifty-three enemy divisions within France and the Low Countries.

The final invasion preparations approved by General Eisenhower called for an assault force with a landing strength of six reinforced divisions, plus three airborne divisions. To the east, the Second British Army would attack initially with three infantry divisions and a brigade of the Sixth British Airborne Division, which was responsible for securing the main bridges over the Orne River between Caen and the English Channel. The First U.S. Army, commanded by Lt. Gen. Omar N. Bradley, was responsible for two assault areas—Omaha and Utah beaches.

The mission of the V Corps, under the command of Maj. Gen. Leonard T. Gerow, with the First Infantry Division as the initial assault force, was to secure the Omaha beachhead between Port-en-Bessin and the Vire River. The V Corps was to receive early reinforcement by elements of the Twenty-ninth Infantry Division and also was strongly reinforced by artillery, armor, and engineers, plus two battalions of Army Rangers.

Utah beach was assigned to the VII Corps, commanded by Maj. Gen. J. Lawton Collins. To carry out his mission, Collins was assigned two airborne divisions, the Eighty-second and the 101st, and the initial assault unit, the Fourth Infantry Division, commanded by Maj. Gen. Raymond O. Barton. Collins' follow-up division was the Ninetieth Infantry Division with Brig. Gen. Jay W. MacKelvie in command.

"Lightning Joe" Collins, a dynamic, driving, and aggressive commander seasoned with battle experience in the Pacific theater, issued his initial VII Corps order in the Spring of 1944:

Eighty-second Airborne Division: Secure west edge of Corps bridgehead, capture Ste. Mère-Eglise; establish deep bridgehead over Merderet River on two main roads west from Ste. Mère-Eglise to support drive to St. Sauveur-le-Vicomte.
101st Airborne Division: Seize area Pont l'Abbé north to west of Gourbesville; east to Beuzeville; south to beyond Ste. Mère-Eglise; west to Chef-du-Pont; continue west to Pont l'Abbé.
Fourth Infantry Division: Assault Utah beach at H-Hour; establish a beachhead; drive on Cherbourg.
Ninetieth Infantry Division: Land D+1 and +2; move

inland to assigned area; regroup with a view of moving
rapidly to north of Sinope River; in conjunction with the
Fourth Infantry Division, capture Cherbourg.

Cherbourg was the key to the mission of the VII Corps.
Collins and Bradley knew the assault forces plus those that would
reinforce the First Army could not logistically be supported for
any duration with over-the-beach delivery techniques. With an
infantry division in World War II requiring seven hundred tons
of supplies a day, the First Army had to have deep-water port
facilities.

Another critical objective to the Normandy campaign was
to prevent the Germans from reinforcing their defensive units on
the Cotentin Peninsula. Toward that end, the 101st was to secure
routes off the beach as the Eighty-second protected the initial
beach landings and sealed off the base of the assault forces on the
peninsula.

Immediately facing Utah beach was a regiment of the
German 709th Division and a mixture of anticommunist Russians, Georgians, Estonians, and others.

The Seventh German Army had the capability of immediate counterattack as well as reinforcing prepared defensive
positions. The recently arrived Ninety-first and the 243rd Divisions were poised to respond to the landings, along with the 352nd
Division, which was conducting maneuvers in the Omaha beach
area. Additionally, the landing forces faced heavy ground defenses. Artillery and mortar fire observation generally was limited because of the ubiquitous hedgerows of the *bocage* country.
Strong beach fortifications included pill boxes, tank and personnel mines, tank traps, and mobile weaponry, as well as field
fortifications sited with the unerring eye of German gunners.
Another factor was the intentional flooding of the lowlands by the
Germans, which had restricted vehicle and foot movement to
causeways off the beach. The Germans knew Normandy's terrain.

The first elements of the U.S. airborne divisions of the VII
Corps—members of the Eighty-second and 101st pathfinder

teams—touched French soil at H-Hour minus five hours. These teams soon were followed by 16,000 Americans using parachutes and gliders in order to completely envelope that portion of Hitler's Atlantic Wall in the Normandy area of Utah beach.

The U.S. Fourth Infantry Division, reinforced with two infantry battalions of the Ninetieth Infantry Division (First and Third Battalions, 359th Infantry), came ashore beginning at 0630 hours on June 6th. The Fourth Division's Eighth Infantry Regiment was put ashore by the Navy some 2,000 yards southeast of the intended beach. This proved fortunate, for the unintended landing area was well out of range of a gun emplacement that could have wracked the wading soldiers if they had landed in the planned area. Brig. Gen. Teddy Roosevelt quickly recognized the landing error and, under occasional enemy small-arms fire, nonchalantly directed the misplaced soldiers to their assigned tactical positions. For this particular act of bravery he received the Medal of Honor, posthumously, following his untimely death by a heart attack during the night of 13 July 1944.

6 June. D-day: The main body of the division sailed from Bristol Channel for the coast of France. Group A (1st and 3rd Battalions of the 359th Infantry Regiment) landed on Utah Beach at 1000–1600 hours and moved to the assembly area in the vicinity of St. Martin de Varreville as part of the 4th Infantry Division's Reserve.[1]

7 June. D+1: Group A moved to an assembly area in the vicinity of Reuville. The *Susan B. Anthony*, which carried the division's advance detachment and the 2nd Battalion of the 359th Infantry Regiment, struck a mine off Utah Beach and sank in approximately two hours. All men were saved, but the bulk of the equipment other than individual was lost. Elements of the 2nd Battalion, 359th, assembled by nightfall. The remainder of the division sailed eastward along the coast of England.

Brig. Gen. Samuel T. Williams undoubtedly was the only American general who, during the first hours of the invasion, stood off Omaha and landed on Utah beaches. He and others of the advanced detachment were among the last to be taken off the sinking *Anthony* by the British gunboat *Nedbrough*. Typically, he urged the boat captain to signal other rescue vessels to follow him to Utah. None did so, and he ended up at Omaha where he reported to General Collins by radio. Collins, aboard the *Bayfield* located off Utah, ordered LCMs to pick up the survivors on the *Nedbrough* and deliver them to Utah. When Williams arrived there, he immediately ordered the armed soldiers to report to the 359th while the unarmed were moved to the division command post, which was located a mile west of Audouville.

Capt. O. C. Talbott (later General) was with General Williams during the sinking of the *Anthony* and the delivery to Omaha by the *Nedbrough*. He recalls that General Williams was active and decisive during the lengthy day: "Just prior to my departure after arriving on Utah he shook my hand, thanked me for my assistance, and became almost emotional as he bade me goodbye. I am convinced that he felt we would never see each other again. We did not know each other well, but he was a bit sentimental."[2]

Another officer, Lt. Col. James O. Boswell (later Brigadier General), the Ninetieth G2, remembers General Williams in a different light: "When we first met on the beach, he asked to borrow my map for he had lost his somewhere along the way." Boswell was reluctant to give him his map, for it was as much a part of him as his pistol or his toothbrush. But he did, and regretted it: "He never returned that map and it always annoyed me. I had colored every key terrain feature on that map and was absolutely familiar with every foot of ground it depicted in the Utah area. Try as I did, I never got that map back."[3]

Taking Boswell's map along, General Williams visited the command posts of the VII Corps and the Fourth Division, along with Colonel C.K. Fales, the 359th's commander. He exchanged information and briefed Maj. Gen. Eugene M. Landrum, the deputy commanding general of the VII, on the current situation with his advance detachment, the sinking of the *Susan B. Anthony*, and the need to obtain weapons for the soldiers who had lost theirs during the sinking.

The principal members of the advance detachment were directed to conduct personal reconnaissances and to contact units of the Eighty-second Airborne located in the area. Williams reminded them of the forthcoming mission of the Ninetieth "to attack to the north in conjunction with the Fourth and seize Cherbourg."

General Williams returned to VII Corps command post during the late hours of June 7th for a conference with General Landrum, who surprised him with the information that the Ninetieth's mission was going to change. The progress of the Eighty-second Airborne Division and the Fourth Infantry Division was slower than had been expected, and Bradley and Collins felt that the Cotentin Peninsula had to be sealed on the east and south to deny opportunity to the Germans to counterattack and possibly destroy the two shallow bridgeheads over the Merderet River.

> **8 June. D+2:** The main body of the Division arrived off Utah Beach at mid-morning and began debarkation from all three transports simultaneously at 1200. By midnight, all foot elements had closed into allocated positions in the division's Assembly Area—Turqueville, Reuville, Audouville, La Hubert, Ecoqueneauville—with the Division CP set up at the village of Loutres. Only 5% of the Division's transport vehicles were available because *MT* ship unloading was far behind schedule. The Division Commander received warning orders that the 90th Infantry Division would attack across the Merderet River through the lines of the 82nd Airborne Division with a view to cutting off the Peninsula. The 359th Infantry moved by battalion to the vicinity of Baudienville, still part of the 4th Infantry Division's Reserve.

At first light on the morning of June 8th, General Williams, using Boswell's map and accompanied by 1st Lt. Carl Everett, his aide, made a detailed survey of the area he expected the division to move across toward the high ground east of the Douve River. To capture the division objective, it would be necessary to cross the Merderet at Chef-du-Pont and La Fière, over unsecured bridges and causeways that would continue to receive enemy fire through June 12th.

General MacKelvie arrived at the division command post with his staff shortly before noon after anchoring off St. Marcouf with elements of the 358th Infantry. Colonel Bacon and General Williams briefed him and his staff on the change of mission. He appeared to be slightly disturbed by the new approach to cut off the peninsula at the base, as he and the G3, Lt. Col. Richard G. Stilwell, made a hurried reconnaissance along the east banks of the Merderet River.

During the afternoon of the 8th, General Williams worked closely with members of the staff as they planned the Ninetieth's second attack order. MacKelvie, according to one observer, sat in a room of the French farmhouse that was the division command post and stared into the distance. Perhaps the change in the Ninetieth's mission disturbed him, who, as an artilleryman, was unfamiliar with the art of infantry command. His strong points were in algebraic functions, logarithm tables, firing charts, and the displacement of field pieces. His military training had not taught him the importance of command adaptability and the need for quick adjustment to battlefield situations. Meditate, and perhaps, sulk he did.

General Williams carried the completed Ninetieth attack plan to VII Corps and then visited the 357th and 358th Regiments to explain the mission and the operational changes to Colonel J.V. Thompson, commanding officer of the 358th, and Col. P.D. Ginder of the 357th. He then talked to Brig. Gen. John M. Devine, commanding officer of Ninetieth artillery, whom he commended for the speed he demonstrated in getting elements of the Ninetieth Artillery to support the Eighty-second Airborne.

9 June. D+3: Infantry and Engineer reconnaissance parties were dispatched by the Division to reconnoiter possible crossing sites along the Merderet River within the contemplated zone of action. Particular attention was paid to the bridges opposite the towns of Chef-du-Pont, Les Dupres, and Grainville. Corps order gave the Division the mission of attacking to the West on 10 June to seize the high ground East of the Douve in the vicinity of St. Sauveur-le-Vicomte to deepen the Corps bridgehead. 359th was still to remain attached to the 4th Infantry Division. During the day, the 82nd Airborne Division, supported by the 345th FA Battalion of the 90th Infantry Division, drove a bridgehead across the Merderet River at 308910. It was determined that the crossing at Chef-du-Pont was lightly held. The situation in the vicinity of Grainville remained obscure. By 1800 the bulk of the Division's equipment had been put ashore, and shortly before dark, the 90th Division was set in motion toward jump-off positions for the morning. A new CP was chosen at 2200. In the meantime, elements of 359 were employed by the 4th Infantry Division to mop up bypassed resistance and to make a reconnaissance in force within its sector. The 2nd Battalion was only 50% equipped as a result of the loss during the sinking.

The completed plan as approved by MacKelvie was nearly an army field manual example of tactical and administrative expertise. It called for a hasty attack that allowed subordinate commanders—Thompson of the 358th and Ginder of the 357th—maximum freedom to use available fire power and maneuver room. Although the enemy dispositions and counterattack capabilities were not completely known, information given to the Ninetieth by the Eighty-second Airborne was adequate. The lack of the third regiment, the 359th, which continued to be attached to the Fourth Division, was a weak point, but one that was dictated by the circumstances of the VII Corps operation.

The terrain was, at the time of the Ninetieth's attack, favorable to the operation. Cover and concealment was available for use throughout the planned avenues of forward movement; observation was poor, making tactical control of small units difficult. The information garnered from the Eighty-second Airborne lacked any tactical information related to the hedgerows west of the Merderet. The slightly elevated terrain south of the Merderet provided identifiable intermediate objectives that, upon capture, would contribute to the final effort to seize the high ground above the Douve, a line that was generally a trace extending from St. Sauveur-le-Vicomte, Ste. Colombe, and Terre-de-Beauval.

10 June. D+4: Upon order of Corps, the Division attacked on 10 June 1944 with the object of seizing the high ground East of the Douve River. Plans called for two regiments to attack abreast, take an intermediate objective, and then push on to the final goal. The 358th Infantry was assigned the left sector of the drive and the 357th Infantry the right sector. The remainder of the 358th was placed in Division Reserve to be prepared to advance in either of the regimental zones. The Division Artillery was ordered to prepare to mass its fires in either of the regimental zones, while the normal support battalions were to render support to their respective Infantry Regiments. 359th remained attached to the 4th Infantry Division. Both Infantry Regiments crossed the LD at the prescribed time (the 358th at 0400 and the 357th at 0515). The 358th successfully crossed the Merderet River and after severe resistance reduced a chateau that was occupied by the Germans. The 357th advanced in its zones of action and encountered enemy resistance in the vicinity of the town of Amfreville. The 358th's elements made an attempt to capture Etienville, but strong German counterattack forced a platoon that had entered the town to withdraw. Fighting slowed down at 2300. Verbal orders were given to continue the attack the following day.

MacKelvie and Williams were with Thompson when the First Battalion, 358th, under the command of Lt. Col. William L. "Spike" Nave, crossed the Merderet River west of Chef-du-Pont at 0400 hours. Earlier, heavy artillery fire had been concentrated on a chateau compound between the causeway leading to Pont l'Abbé and the juncture of the Douve and the Merderet rivers. Nave drove to the village of Picauville with little loss of men or momentum. As the First Battalion continued forward, it met strong opposition from prepared positions west of Picauville.

At that time, MacKelvie ordered a part of the division reserve to the right of the First Battalion as part of Colonel Thompson's attacking element. Thompson became nervous about some scattered small-arms fire coming from a chateau area, and he directed Company I to clear it. The southern progress of the regiment stopped, and in the late afternoon hours, Colonel

Thompson directed the two forward battalions to "dig in."

In the division's western front, the 357th made a passage of Eighty-second Airborne lines at the La Fière bridge under heavy German artillery fire. The enemy fire delayed the advance of the leading Second Battalion, which was followed by the Third. One attacking battalion lost its commander at the first crack of German small-arms fire. Untouched by it but claiming "eyesight failure," the commander was evacuated to the relative safety and comfort of the rear area. The battalion's executive officer assumed command, and he was killed leading his soldiers two days after the battalion had been abandoned by its lieutenant colonel.

The 357th did not distinguish itself after crossing the Merderet, for its movement ahead was stopped above Le Motey less than a mile west of the bridge and causeway. Hill 30 at Le Motey was held by elements of the Eighty-second Airborne. The attempts by both the Second and Third Battalions in the afternoon to reach Amfreville went unrewarded. The first day of combat resulted in fifteen soldiers killed and eighty-four wounded—the price paid by the 357th for unsuccessfully trying to capture the intermediate objective.

11 June. D+5: Both Regiments, supported by effective artillery barrage, continued to press the attack in their respective sectors during the day. The 358th, with two battalions abreast, made an assault against the town of Pont l'Abbé (Etienville) from the East. One battalion served as a holding force on the northwest side of the town. The Division Artillery supported this attack. The 359th (less one battalion) was released from assignment to the 4th Infantry Division and reverted to the control of the 90th Division on 10 June. It moved to an alert area and was committed to action in the vicinity of Picauville to the east of Pont l'Abbé. Units of the Regiment received a severe shelling during the move to that sector. By nightfall, the entire Regiment had been committed. Elsewhere, the units adjusted their lines and made preparation for a continuation of the attack on the morrow.

General Williams got little sleep or rest for the next three days, spending every waking minute at the front with the forward battalions of the 357th and the 358th. Whenever the attack of a particular battalion appeared to be making progress, he would hurry to another. He knew through radio reports and contact with the division G3 that Lieutenant Colonel Stilwell was having a difficult time.

During his visits, General Williams was quick to assist battalion and company commanders with the accomplishment of their missions, but he did not interfere directly with their plans or countermand their orders. He encouraged greater use of the Ninetieth's artillery and the battalion's eighty-one-millimeter mortars. He helped company commanders with ammunition resupply, evacuation of the wounded, and establishment of wire and radio communication. He insisted that the battalion commanders make their presence known to the frontline riflemen of their unit, for he knew it was the ordinary soldier who would carry the day for the Ninetieth. Frequently, he visited rear-area medical facilities, but the sound of artillery fire and the chatter of machine guns held his immediate attention. Once, he strongly rebuked the Ninetieth's chief of staff, Col. Robert L. Bacon, who appeared to him to be unaggressive and indecisive in accomplishing his responsibilities of clearing the area of dead and severely wounded soldiers.

Yet despite the example Williams set, the battle continued to favor the Germans because of their masterful use of hedgerows as defensive works. He personally interviewed many prisoners, always trying to find a solution to defeat the German's unexpected superiority gained by their use of the French hedgerows.

The progress of the attacking regiments, including the 359th (less its First Battalion), was measured in feet. The division was a failure. It did not exhibit the strength or, unfortunately, the will to accomplish its mission to seize the high ground east of the Douve River.

12 June. D+6: The two regiments continued to push forward upon the opening of the new day. The 357th Infantry pressed its attack at 0800 with the mission of capturing the high ground in the vicinity of Amfreville. It then planned to reorganize and attack in the general direction of Gourbesville.

The 358th Infantry continued its attack on Pont l'Abbé with the plan of eventually pushing on to occupy the high ground beyond the town. The 359th Infantry was kept in readiness for Division Reserve. The 357th Infantry fought fiercely throughout the day, but due to the ferocity of the enemy, they were able to make very little gain. The 358th Infantry encountered severe resistance in its sector and was forced to press the enemy back in hedgerow-to-hedgerow combat. American planes bombed Pont l'Abbé at 1700. Their attack was very effective. It greatly aided the 358th Infantry in its approach to Pont l'Abbé. A coordinated attack preceded by the support of all available artillery was launched on the town at 1900. By 2030, patrols of the 1st and 2nd Battalions had entered the town. By 2130, the two Battalions had mopped it up completely and had begun the move to occupy the high ground to the North and Northwest. At nightfall, and under the cover of darkness, unit commanders regrouped their forces in preparation for the continuation of the attack on 13 June.

All three regiments continued to attack a determined enemy that refused to give the attackers an inch of ground. Shortly before noon, Colonel Ginder was relieved of his command of the 357th and ordered to the division command post to rest. Col. W. Sheehy assumed command.

After making a hasty reconnaissance, Sheehy moved toward Lieutenant Colonel Kilday's battalion located northeast of Gourbesville. Apparently in great haste, he ordered his jeep driver to follow the Amfreville–Gourbesville road instead of following the trace of forward soldiers of the Third Battalion. He continued toward Kilday's area in his jeep but was stopped by a soldier who told him he was forward of the front lines. Colonel Sheehy then left his vehicle and moved ahead on foot, his jeep following. He encountered devastating machine pistol fire, and his body was later discovered in a German aid station when Gourbesville was finally captured.

MacKelvie then assigned command of the 357th to General Williams, who still functioned also as assistant division commander.

By now in the 358th, Colonel Thompson was badly wounded and evacuated by medical personnel. Lieutenant Colonel Nave was also wounded but after treatment was able to continue as commander of the First Battalion. He also hurriedly took command of the 358th when Thompson was wounded. Unfortunately, he was killed in action two days later. Another battalion commander, Lt. Col. James E. Casey of the Third Battalion 359th, was also slightly wounded and evacuated to the rear.

General Collins visited the 358th and found no senior leaders until he met Lieutenant Colonel Nave northwest of Orglandes. Collins was particularly disturbed by the fact that little enemy small-arms firing was present, and no German artillery was registering or falling. On his return to the division command post, he came upon a group of soldiers of the Ninetieth in a ditch along the side of a main road well back of the front. Collins asked them what they were doing and received an evasive answer. He proceeded to "wave the flag," talking of the grand history of the Ninetieth division. But he took no action other than to report the incident to MacKelvie. Collins later wrote that MacKelvie made no excuses and seemed to be bewildered as to what to do about his division's lack of fight, according to Lt. Col. Eames Yates, aide-de-camp to General Williams.[4]

MacKelvie's dispirited, defeatist attitude, coupled with two days of his bungling and timid command was alien to the driving forcefulness Collins sought in commanders. He decided to talk to General Bradley about the division and its commanding general when he returned to his VII Corps command post.

Meanwhile, as Collins visited the 358th Regiment, General Sam Williams was continuing to fight with the 357th. He did not accomplish much. One of the first actions he ordered was a sweep to the rear of the 357th's zone of action to pick up and return "stragglers" to the regiment. Two officers were given this job. Before nightfall they had discovered more than 180 lost, sometimes cowardly, but most often poorly led and frightened soldiers. Each was ordered to rejoin his company under the supervision of one of the officers.

13 June. D+7: At 0500 the Division continued its attack, concentrating on the capture of the town of Gourbesville. The main attack was preceded by the attempt on the part of a task force consisting of an Engineer Company to capture the town. This failed to materialize due to the severity of the enemy resistance. The 357th Infantry then attempted to force their way forward only to meet strong resistance which lasted throughout the rest of the day. In the 358th's sector, the Division's units were successful in capturing and occupying the high ground to the North and West of Pont l'Abbé. Effective patrolling was conducted by the 359th Infantry, covering a three-mile sector.

General Collins relieved MacKelvie in the morning at the division command post. The following day he wrote to General Bradley:

14 June 1944
Subject: Relief of Division Commander
To: Commanding General, First United States Army

1. Upon oral authority granted by you this date, I have relieved Brigadier General Jay W. MacKelvie from command of the 90th Infantry Division and have replaced him by Major General Eugene M. Landrum.

2. The 90th Division has been in action since 10 June when it passed through a shallow bridge head which had been established by the 82nd Airborne Division west of the Merderet River. The division had the mission of attacking to the west to secure the line of the Douve River south of Terre de Beauval. It made fair progress initially, but during the past three days it has advanced only approximately two thousand yards. I have visited the division each of these days, going to each of the regiments and in many instances to frontline battalions. The enemy opposition, in my opinion, has been relatively light except for mortar and 88-mm Artillery fire. G-2 information indicates that the enemy opposing the 90th Division has consisted of elements of units whose strength is less than one regimental combat team. From what I and my staff officers have observed, it is my belief that this opposition could have been overcome by a vigorous attack.

3. In fairness to Brigadier General MacKelvie, it is my

belief that the 90th Division was not fully prepared for combat and lacked competent leadership in certain of its regiments and battalions and perhaps in lower echelons. I understand that General MacKelvie has only recently assumed command of the division. However, he has not demonstrated his ability to correct existing conditions, perhaps because he lacks familiarity with the problems of infantry combat. While personally brave, he has been unable to instill a determined aggressiveness in his men. I feel that it was mandatory to replace him with an experienced division commander who had already proven his ability in action.

4. General MacKelvie is a competent Artilleryman and I believe that he is still capable of handling the Artillery of a division in action.

J. Lawton Collins
Major General, U.S. Army, Commanding

Major General Landrum assumed command of the division about midday, June 13th. When Sam learned this, he felt sympathetic toward MacKelvie because he had confronted and spoken quite harshly to him the afternoon before. He had found MacKelvie lying prone in a shallow ground furrow, tight against a hedgerow. The sight infuriated Sam, who reportedly said belligerently to him, "Goddamit General, you can't lead this division hiding in that goddam hole. Go back to the CP. Get the hell out of that hole and go to your vehicle. Walk to it, or you'll have this goddam division wading in the English Channel."[5] When told of MacKelvie's relief, Sam wondered if his caustic words had reached Collins.

During the first days of combat in Normandy, Sam showed a change of personality. His usual harshness with commissioned subordinates gave way to a gentleness seldom seen during training. He was especially concerned with the daily welfare of the riflemen and junior officers. His aide, Lieutenant Colonel Yates, affectionately known as Junior, said he observed Sam's mellowing: "We had been engaged for a couple of days when I made a stupid error in preparing his map with the latest information. At Barkley or in the desert this would have marked my end—it would have been suicidal. But in Normandy, I was greatly surprised when he, prior to leaving the division CP, put his arm around my shoulders and said, 'Junior, you know better than that.'"[6]

Sam's attitude toward General MacKelvie also changed. He had been understanding and respectful in the beginning of his association with MacKelvie, but his demeanor in France gave way to abusiveness and disdain. Sam expected his division commander to set an example of courage and bravery for all, but especially so for the junior officers of infantry and artillery who were in the forward areas of battle. General Collins had written of MacKelvie that he was "personally brave," but this statement was believed to be fraudulent according to many witnesses. The death of his aide, Lieutenant Harris, and the continual suffering of the wounded affected MacKelvie to a point that he was of no value as a division commander.

His service had been that of an exemplary staff officer and a competent commander of artillery. Nothing of his army training, however, had prepared him for the carnage on the infantry battlefield. Small-arms fire rattled him; incoming artillery discomposed him; the sight and sounds of the dying frontline soldiers exhausted him. From the beginning on Utah beach, he was useless.

As the battle developed for the Ninetieth, General Williams became appalled at the unnecessary waste of life caused by MacKelvie's incompetency and that of some of the infantry colonels who commanded the division's three regiments. He snarled at Ginder and Thompson for their lack of leadership and for their displays of tactical stupidity. He raged at them for their lack of technical expertise in failing to use the weapons available to them, especially the organic mortars and cannons.

MacKelvie's failure was part of the source of Williams' demeanor, but another failure irritated him—the collective insufficiency of the regimental colonels and particularly some of the lieutenant colonels responsible for leading the nine infantry battalions. With some exceptions, he felt that he had been deceived by these officer subordinates, and especially so by those with whom he had worked in Texas and California. He especially felt a deep responsibility for not having recognized their shallowness and unsuitability for battalion command. Too many of them were officers of little honor. The stark display of a colonel or lieutenant colonel huddling behind available cover, or their miserable comportment in front of soldiers and their unwillingness as leaders to try to move their units forward would forever haunt Sam.

Having had no influence in selecting the middle-level commanders—the lieutenant colonels, the majors, and the colonels—Sam vowed he would never again allow American soldiers to be subjected to the kind of despicable leadership he saw in several of the field-grade officers assigned to the Ninetieth Infantry Division from June 10th through July 16th.

Landrum was an unknown to Sam, but in keeping with his nature and philosophy, he accepted him without qualification. Landrum had the proper military credentials as proved by his service in the Aleutian Islands, where he had commanded an army force for the occupation of an advance base and had accomplished administrative and operational tasks with speed and secrecy. He was awarded the Distinguished Service Medal for his work there, having accomplished his mission and displayed unusual foresight, energy, good judgment, and technical skill while doing so. Later, in July of 1943, Landrum received the U.S. Navy Distinguished Service Medal. He commanded all U.S. forces on the island of Attu from 17 to 31 May 1943. His citation emphasized his eradication of Japanese resistance during the two-week period. Bradley and Collins both thought highly of him and expected him to breathe fire and spirit into the Ninetieth Infantry Division.

Landrum's first combat report to General Bradley was an absurd note that paraphrased World War I French Commander Foch when he said, "My center is giving away and my right flank falls back. All goes well. I am attacking." Landrum told Bradley, "On objective on my right, progressing to objective in the middle, getting nowhere on the left. Will attack again."[7] The report was especially ludicrous because the right intermediate objective was not captured until the evening of June 15th, nor was the first objective assigned to the Ninetieth ever captured by it.

Similarly, Landrum's first message on 14 June to Sam and other commanders, obviously written before he made a terrain analysis or reconnaissance, said, "Tell unit commanders that I have assumed command. My creed is fire and movement. Avoid hard spots and hit the weak. Carry out the orders in your sector you have received."

As General Williams, assistant division commander of the Ninetieth and also presently the commanding officer of the 357th Infantry Regiment, surveyed the ground in front of the 357th, he wondered how he could use "fire and movement" in the labyrinthine hedgerows of the French fields of Gourbesville. The Ninetieth's training and preparation for combat in Texas and elsewhere had been designed to prepare the infantry to take advantage of cover and concealment, capitalize on observed artillery fire, and advance through the use of maneuver and supporting fire. But this philosophy could not be adopted in the hedgerows, which stopped forward movement. Hedgerows are not isolated fields; rather, they define the owner's orchard, crop field, or animal grazing area. Hedgerows, which are sometimes eight feet high, have the intricate design of a spider's web—an interwoven, irregular pattern of piled banks of debris and earth held in place by the growth of trees, brush, and uncultivated vegetation and briars. If a soldier penetrated a hedgerow and lived as he ran across the inside of the field under enemy fire, he would be stopped again at the next field edge by more hedgerows. The Ninetieth had quite a challenge before it in such terrain.

14 June. D+8: Corps order called for elements of the 82nd Airborne Division and the newly arrived 9th Infantry Division to pass through the 90th Division, and 358th Infantry was ordered to make a limited attack in order to mask the move. After elements of the 82nd Airborne Division had passed through satisfactorily, 358th Infantry assembled in the vicinity of Pont l'Abbé to await further orders. The 357th Infantry continued its attack on Gourbesville, while the 359th Infantry was ordered to assume the attack on Orglandes to the northwest. Elements of the 3rd Battalion of the 357th Infantry fought their way into Gourbesville at 2020 and held their control of the town until the next morning.

General Williams once again watched the sun rise from the lines of the 357th. By now, he knew the division was not going to accomplish its first combat mission of capturing the heights of the Douve. Once again he, along with Lieutenant Colonel Kilday, the Third Battalion commander, awaited the arrival of an Air Corps bombing mission in the early hours of daylight. It never materialized because the supporting artillery did not have the proper color of smoke to mark Gourbesville, again the 357th's objective of the day. He and Kilday planned to attack with the full support of a heavy artillery concentration. As the barrages hit the target area, it was discovered that Colonel Ginder, who had been relieved and was presumably resting at the division command post, was moving troops forward and into the artillery target area without anyone's permission. General Williams felt that Ginder's action was costly because unnecessary lives were lost through his unauthorized tactical shifting of troops on the ground east of Gourbesville. Williams placed Colonel Ginder under arrest and returned him to the division command post under armed escort. From that day, Williams showed nothing but contempt for Ginder by ignoring him at every opportunity.

Once again, along with General Devine, Williams and Kilday planned another attack on Gourbesville. Williams, although not assuming command of Kilday's battalion, closely supervised Kilday's actions and gave persuasive suggestions that Kilday followed in detail.

At 2115 hours, the attack began with infantrymen closely following a heavy artillery concentration. Williams moved to the south with the right assault company toward Gourbesville. As he advanced, he assisted the small-unit leaders by directing their attention to fire coming from Gourbesville and encouraging them to cover the German fire with their own rifle fire. The right elements of the leading units of the Third Battalion faltered and took cover behind a stone wall when they should have continued forward. At that time, Williams aggressively and actively told the riflemen to follow him to the center and beyond the town. General Williams continued to lead the rifle units and, completely disregarding his own safety from intense enemy small-arms fire, stepped into the center of a road and engaged the enemy with his carbine. He yelled to the soldiers to move forward with him and led them through the center of the village, firing his carbine as he advanced. Designating enemy targets and directing fire to them, he continued forward with the assault unit until joined by other squads of the leading platoon.

Several years later, General Williams would receive the Silver Star for his demonstrated personal bravery, leadership, and gallantry, all of which led in June of 1944 to the capture of a demolished pile of rubble named Gourbesville, along with its important road network.

Gourbesville, an intermediate objective since June 10th, was captured and held, finally, by Gen. Sam Williams and the 357th Infantry on June 15th.

(Next page) Maj. Gen. Eugene M. Landrum, commanding general, Ninetieth Infantry Division, Normandy, France, 1944. Sam's and Landrum's personalities clashed, and Landrum eventually requested Sam's reduction.

Chapter 7 ☆ ☆ ☆ *Normandy, July 1944*

General Landrum, within hours after taking command of the Ninetieth, received orders to help the Eighty-second and the newly arrived Ninth Divisions pass through the Ninetieth's lines. General Collins directed both of these units to attack west and seize what had once been the Ninetieth's objective—the line of the Douve. The Eighty-second was to take St. Sauveur-le-Vicomte in the south, and the Ninth was to seize Ste. Colombe.

The Ninetieth received a new mission after the other divisions had cleared the area. Collins directed it to move to the north and occupy and hold a defensive line that would protect the north flank of the Ninth from Montebourg and westward to Terre-de-Beauval on the Douve.

On the morning of June 14th, the 358th attacked from its position in the vicinity of Pont l'Abbé and secured a road junction above the village. From there, the 507th Parachute Infantry and the 325th Glider Infantry began their movement west. By midnight, both units had advanced less than a mile under heavy enemy fire of every description. Early in the evening, a counterattack pushed the 507th's right back several hundred yards.

The Sixtieth Infantry Regiment of the Ninth Division attacked through the lines of the 359th, but its movement also was slow, advancing only as far as the two regiments of the Eighty-second.

The next two days of combat were favorable for the two divisions attacking to the Douve. By 2400 hours on June 16th, they were in charge of their objectives and were on the way to the sea on the Cotentin's south shore. General of the Artillery Wilhelm Fahrmbacher of the German LXXXIV Corps had reported to his army headquarters on June 14th that a large-scale attack by the Americans could not be held because the units were split and the troops were tired and had insufficient ammunition. On the same day, Col. Benjamin A. Dickson told General Bradley: "The Boche is pulling out. They have conceded us the [Cotentin] peninsula." When he had taken command of the Ninetieth, Landrum had flippantly promised General Bradley "a salt water cocktail from the other side of the Cotentin."[1]

However admirable the successes of the two divisions that cut the Cotentin, there is little cause to measure the failures of the Ninetieth by the victories of others. From June 10th through June 14th, the Ninetieth had been fighting Germans who had no intention of withdrawing, unlike the weakened enemy forces that faced the Eighty-second and the Ninth.

The Ninetieth Infantry Division, in moving to its new location, never lost contact with the enemy. By June 18th, the division had occupied its defensive line, organized it for battle, replenished its supplies, and licked its wounds, which were serious. On June 18th, the Ninetieth was assigned to the VII Corps, commanded by Maj. Gen. Troy H. Middleton.

For the next twelve days, the division would continue to defend its wide sector. The relative quiet area provided the regimental commanders time to reorganize and conduct limited training. But the division was badly mauled, exhausted, and disheartened, and was short of small-unit leaders and devoid of spirit and pride.

As the Ninetieth moved to the defensive line, General Bradley assigned two replacement regimental commanders to the division. Col. Richard C. Partridge, a 1920 West Point graduate, was placed in command of the 358th after Thompson was wounded. Although Partridge was an artillery officer, Collins had spoken confidently to Bradley about his background and qualifications. Later, after his recovery from a serious wound, Partridge would become the chief of staff of the VII Corps. The other new commander was Col. George B. Barth, who was also a Military Academy graduate and an artillery officer. Colonel Fales of the 359th would continue to command until July 6th when another colonel, Robert Bacon, was given the 359th. After the war had ended, Colonel Barth (later Major General) wrote:

I joined the Ninetieth Division on 16 June and was assigned to command the 357th Infantry. At that time, the division had been in action for about a week and had been badly smashed up. The day prior to my assignment, two of the regimental commanders had become casualties. One [Sheehy] was killed; the second [Thompson] was wounded. I joined my regiment early the next morning. I had never before experienced "zero morale." The officers in my new headquarters seemed for the most part very competent but were absolutely sunk. I realized that I had a situation where I would have to start from the bottom and rebuild the organization, particularly with regard to morale and their confidence as soldiers. I took my S3 and immediately made a reconnaissance of our front. At that time, another regiment had taken over the front line. On the way back we passed a long column of troops. I asked the S3 what battalion that was. His reply was, "those are our replacements." They totaled I believe about 800 men. This gives a general picture of the number of casualties sustained by the regiment after their first week of fighting, since almost all the casualties were from the rifle and heavy weapons companies.

I decided to visit each battalion and talk to the assembled officers. Everywhere there was gloom and discouragement. I had prepared a large map, which I brought with me when I came to the regiment (I was previously chief of staff of the Ninth Division). This showed the "big picture," indicating all of the divisions ashore and their missions. I explained to the officers that the Ninetieth had had the toughest job of all in that they were fighting the German troops in prepared defensive positions while the Eighty-second and Ninth Divisions executed an envelopment to cut the Cotentin Peninsula and allow us to advance on Cherbourg. I stressed the fact that while the Ninetieth had had terribly heavy casualties, their job had been highly important and that if they had not fought hard and held the Germans in positions, the enveloping attack, which at that time was well on the way to success, would have been a failure. After I gave this picture, I could see signs of encouragement and understanding in the faces of many of the officers.

I was very fortunate in having two very fine staff officers at regimental headquarters, Capt. William DePuy as S3 and 1st Lt. Charles W. Ryder, Jr., as S2, who were able to give me honest opinions on the sort of performance I could expect of the battalions. I realized that this practice would not normally be good and that an officer, being asked to evaluate a fellow officer, particularly if senior to him, would be reluctant to give me the truth. However, I had the feeling that these staff officers, realizing the terrible condition of the regiment and deciding above all else that the regiment must retrieve itself, would give me support and furnish honest answers. I took no immediate action on anything they told me but made notes for later verification by my personal observation.

After returning to my headquarters from this series of conferences, I felt that the next crying need was to find out, first hand, the techniques of the German defense in hedgerow country. To get this information, I had two battalion commanders go with me over the ground where their troops had been in combat, and we tried to reconstruct the pattern of German defense that had been so devastating to us. The regiment had made an advance of about two miles just before I joined. This allowed me free access to these battlefield areas. As a result of this study, we hastily prepared a paper on German defense methods, circulated it through the command, and I ordered that during the period when we were not actually in the line, each battalion would conduct schools for officers and have practical small problems of attack in hedgerow country. Since it was only a matter of days until we would be fighting again, we took this method to get some benefit from our past mistakes and to increase the competence of the men in overcoming the very specialized German defense in hedgerows.[2]

Similar conditions to those described for the 357th Infantry Regiment existed also in other regiments, such as the 358th and the 359th: poor morale, lack of leadership, loss of confidence in some leaders, and failing unit spirit.

During this period, General Williams was as active as ever. After he woke each morning, he would immediately go to the G3 tent and study the situation map and all messages that had come in since his last visit, which usually would have been well after midnight. He would question the G3 duty officer as to any extraordinary activity. The duty sergeant would serve him a cup of hot coffee, which would be his only nourishment for the next six hours. When he had finished this visit, Williams would return to his billet for about thirty minutes. When he emerged, he would be neatly dressed and would move with the bearing of a confident, assured general.

For the next thirteen days, Williams spent his time before sunrise, during the hours of daylight, and well beyond sunset either where he had been ordered to visit, or at the point of danger at the division's front. He visited every regiment at least once a day, joined the frontline battalion of attacking units at the company level, studied the effectiveness of fire support units located behind the frontline platoons, conferred with the members of the 315th Engineers closest to the front, followed the progress of battle elsewhere over radio nets of divisional units, and educated elements of tankers and antiaircraft units as to their role of support. In a letter dated 10 August 1944, he wrote to Lt. Gen. Ben Lear:

During this period [from D+1 until 15 July 1944] my duties consisted entirely of outside work, as contrasted to work at division headquarters . . . it was necessary that daily I be at the most important place or places on the division front, assisting . . . regimental battalion commanders in leading their troops in the assault. For a few days in the latter part of June, I commanded the 357th Infantry in action due to the enforced sick absence of the regimental commander. [Colonel Barth had been hospitalized for a carbuncle removal.] There was no day during this period that I did not visit, advise, and assist one or more regimental and battalion commanders.

After the capture of Cherbourg by the VII Corps, the Ninetieth began preparations to attack south from areas well-known to the division's leadership. Its three regiments were moved to assembly areas located within what had been the division's zone of action a month earlier. The Ninetieth on the left would join the Eighty-second Airborne in the center and the Seventy-ninth to attack and seize the ground immediately north of Lessay and Périers.

Three German divisions, the Second SS Panzer, the Seventy-seventh Infantry, and the 353rd Infantry, were in well-prepared defensive works that extended from La Haye du Puits to Carentan on the east. Dominating the area was the formidable Hill 122, on the southern slopes of which was located the Forêt de Mont Castre. The Germans had maximum observation of the areas from which the VIII Corps would attack, and during the ensuing days they would use this observation to direct killing fire on the American infantrymen as they valiantly moved forward while trying to climb the heights of Mont Castre. Two other obstacles hampered movement in the Ninetieth's left offensive zone: the Prairies Marecageuses, which were a combination of swamp, bog, standing water, and cultivated fields of rice, each inundated with water; and the network of hedgerows, a natural defensive barrier already well-known to the survivors of the battlefields around Chef-du-Pont, La Fière, and Gourbesville.

The Germans recognized the defensive nature of the hedgerow and used them to their great advantage: they had constructed routes through them and had dug off-setting protective dens used for safety, weapons, ammunition storage, and sleeping areas. Above Utah beach, hedgerows again became an integral factor in the defense of what became known as the

Mahlman line. The fields were mined, booby trapped, and inter-locked with supporting bands of machine gun fire and preplanned concentrations of direct and high-angle mortar and artillery fire.

Lt. Col. Chet Hansen, aide and diarist for Gen. Bradley, wrote in Bradley's diary on July 13th: "Hedgerow fighting has been far more difficult than Bradley anticipated." Commanders at all levels, including Bradley, were unprepared to fight their units in the *bocage* country. No training literature that addressed the terrain of Normany had been prepared and distributed by any major command. Later, after General Williams' relief, Bradley would note: "We are far behind in our schedule but schedules did not take into consideration the great difficulties in this *bocage* country with its thick hedgerows. As it is, the country alone makes it far more rough going than we had originally anticipated. Swamps have canalized our movements, particularly in the VIII Corps, up along the western coastline. Where these swamps have restricted movements, attacks have progressed slowly and with-out too apparent success."[3]

The division attacked at 0530 on July 3rd, after a fifteen-minute artillery preparation delivered by the combined weapons of the Fourth and Ninetieth artilleries plus the heavy weapons of the 357th Infantry. The Ninetieth's mission was to smash and penetrate the Mahlman line, which extended from Beau Cour-dray on the east to Forêt de Mont Castre and then to the coast. The 359th on the right was ordered to seize and consolidate Forêt de Mont Castre, while the 358th on the left was to advance through the area between Mont Castre and the Prairies Marecageuses. The 357th, in division reserve, was to be prepared to pass, on order, through the 358th and seize the division objective.

The Germans did not cooperate. They stayed where they were, willing to defend to death their assigned defense sectors. By the end of the day's fighting, the Ninetieth Division had suffered 600 casualties and was able to show a meager gain toward the final objective of 1,200 yards: two yards for each soldier wounded or dead.

The other VIII Corps divisions also did not do well. The Eighty-second on the Ninetieth's right maintained equal gains, but the Seventy-ninth reported little advance. After making some good initial progress, they were stopped when they made contact with the Mahlman line outposts. All divisions reported heavy casualties.

Nor did the VII Corps demonstrate quick victories. There were no easily staked objectives in the *bocage* country. Collins continued placing heavy demands on the unit commanders in spite of having run into the toughest defenses he would face as a corps commander. The French countryside, with its natural obstacles defended by dedicated Germans, had stopped two experienced corps commanders—Middleton and Collins. Middleton wrote, "It took eight days of the hardest fighting to push the Germans off the heights and to move five miles with the Seventy-ninth alone taking more than 2,000 casualties." Apologetically, as he so often did in explaining his corps' shortcomings, he added, "Rain complicated matters, depriving the Americans of air support."[4] He failed to mention the terrain and the enemy.

Collins' divisions advanced even less. For example, his Eighty-third Division attacked at first light on July 4th, with two regiments abreast. "Leadership all through the division [the 83rd] was uncertain. It [the 83rd] fell on its face," Bradley's diary notes. "Collins rushed up elements of Barton's 4th Division, but these units, with a high proportion of replacements did no better. . . . Nor did Eddy's 9th Division when it reached the front on July 9. The VII Corps failed to provide the breakout."[5]

The Germans clearly mastered the battleground because of their brilliant use of the terrain, high-angle fire, and timely use of counterattack units. Also, their attackers experienced poor observation conditions.

The 357th Infantry under Colonel Barth had rough going from the beginning of the attack. The regiment on July 7th had attacked with the First Battalion on the left and the Third on the right, both located on the division's left. Almost immediately, the reinforced Germans hit Barth with strong paratroop counterattacking forces. Companies I and L, supported by tanks, continued their forward progress in spite of the heavy opposition. When they reached a piece of ground that afforded good fields of fires, they stopped momentarily to reorganize before continuing the attack. Once again, they were hit with a counterattack, which they defeated largely by the use of artillery. The First Battalion was roughly handled too, having been driven back to their line of departure. With the First failing to make any progress and returning to its starting point, the Germans once again counterattacked and managed to isolate Companies I and L. Leaderless, they were cut off, yet they fought repeated enemy attempts to infiltrate their positions.

The two decimated companies of the Third Battalion were left to their own devices to remain alive, and the brave isolated attempts by a few to return to the safety of the rear were met with little success. The heavy German artillery and unrelenting tank attacks against hastily occupied defensive positions were successful. Fewer than fifty soldiers of the two companies returned on July 9th to the Ninetieth's lines. The regiment, after attacking for four days, had lost more than 800 officers and men. Barth had little or no reserve, and his Second Battalion was held by Landrum as division reserve.

When General Williams returned to the division command post in the late hours of July 7th, he immediately joined Lt. Col. Stilwell in the G3 section. There he saw a symbol on the situation map that indicated that the Third Battalion of the 357th was surrounded. Stilwell told him that two companies of the 357th had been isolated and that he believed the entire Third Battalion was ineffective. Communication with the the companies was sporadic, and returnees reported harrowing details: soldiers were being annihilated, their officers were wounded or dead, and some infantrymen were throwing their weapons aside and surrendering.

General Williams was furious. During training in 1943 at the California Desert Maneuver area, while briefly having temporary command of the division, he had promised the Ninetieth soldiers and officers that if they were ever cut off, he would commit troops to their rescue. When Williams further learned that Landrum knew of Barth's reserve situation and was aware of the need to commit the division reserve, he became infuriated, stormed to Landrum's location, and dismissed everyone within hearing range. He heatedly condemned Landrum, slashing him for his basement-style leadership and scalding him for his responsibility for the many unnecessary deaths that his "Goddam stupidity" had caused since his assumption of command.[6]

After leaving Landrum, Williams continued to fume to Yates and Everett. He told them what he had yelled at Landrum, and unfortunately for Williams' career, Landrum overheard these strong comments to his aides. With that outburst, Williams marked the beginning of his end as the assistant division commander, Ninetieth Infantry Division, and took the first step toward becoming a colonel of infantry once again.

But General Williams' anger at Landrum was not isolated. Bradley soon realized that Landrum was incapable of effective leadership, believing that Landrum had not "cleaned house enough."[7] He felt compelled to relieve him as soon as he could find a successor.

Major General Landrum was unknown to the soldiers of the Ninetieth Division who were doing the fighting and all-too-often the dying. Landrum, if he had been a battle leader, would have been at the front where he could have seen the situation in Barth's regiment. Had he been near, he would have realized the necessity to commit the division reserve to salvage those soldiers still alive in the cut-off area. Landrum, however, preferred the security of a chateau basement from where he could dictate messages and process paper. Colonel Barth at the time said, "I had lost confidence in Landrum, and he had no confidence in us."[8]

Landrum's fate was sealed when his division in July failed to equal MacKelvie's performance, which had been at best marginal. It was also difficult for Bradley to continue with Landrum in view of his discovery that Landrum rarely went to the front, and certainly did not visit a point of danger. Bradley noted in his diary concerning Landrum: "Every time I went to see him, he was in his command post, which was usually in the basement of some building. He never got outside of it. And he had no way to inspire his division. You got to get out and show you are interested and are willing to take a chance with them."[9]

General Bradley began his search for Landrum's successor from within his own officer resources. Ted Roosevelt and Raymond S. McLain seemed to satisfy Bradley's requirements for a proven leader of men. They were both qualified and able officers, but Bradley favored Roosevelt because he had performed beyond the call of duty since the day he had landed on Utah beach as a spare general with the Fourth Infantry Division. Roosevelt got the nod over McLain because Bradley knew that he would instill confidence and motivation in the Ninetieth. With a thick-skinned disciplinarian as his second in command, Bradley felt the Ninetieth would be a winner over the Germans in a couple of weeks. Bradley never specifically mentioned Sam Williams as being Roosevelt's second, but the fact remains that even in those days, Sam had the reputation as a tough, straightlaced army disciplinarian, and he was the Ninetieth's assistant division commander. But Bradley's selection was not to be; Roosevelt died in his tent on July 13th, so McLain was then chosen.

After Sam's heated discussion with Landrum, their relationship was distant and cool. The antipathy was further kindled a week later after a brief meeting between Sam and Brig. Gen. Don Stroh, commanding general of the Eighth Infantry Division, during which Stroh told Sam that he hesitated to push the Eighth hard while the Ninetieth was in such a weakened condition. Stroh had asked Sam, "Are you people doing any better now?" Sam did not deny to Landrum later, and in a most forceful manner, that he took exception to Stroh's insinuation. He lost his temper and became ill-mannered. Then Landrum told Sam that, in the future, he should avoid similar comments to other senior officers. Sam ended the confrontation with a request that he be transferred to another division.

On Sunday, July 16th, at 1145 hours, General Sam Williams, while at Company G, 357th outpost, received a message to report to corps headquarters. One hour later he stood before Maj. Gen. Troy H. Middleton, the commanding general, VIII U.S. Army Corps, in his command trailer outside of La Haye du Puits.

(Next page) Col. Samuel T. Williams, commanding officer, Twenty-sixth Infantry Regiment, Bamberg, Germany, 1948. Sam's command of the "Blue Spaders" brought the regiment to a peak of efficiency.

Chapter 8 ☆ ☆ ☆ *Humbled Sam*

General Middleton handed Sam a letter as soon as he reported and said without overture, greeting, or amenity, "read this":

14 July 1944
Subject: Assistant Division Commander
To: Commanding General VIII Corps, A.P.O 308, U.S. Army

1. I request that a Brigadier General with combat experience in this war be assigned to this division as Assistant Division Commander at the earliest practicable time and that the present Assistant Division commander, Brigadier General Sam T. Williams, U.S. Army, be given another assignment.

2. While General Williams has discharged the many specific missions that I have assigned to him promptly, I feel that a general officer of a more optimistic and calming attitude would be more beneficial to this division at this time.

3. I believe that a general officer who was not connected with this division during its training period would be of greater assistance to me in the elimination of the training deficiencies that exist in this division.

E. M. Landrum
Major General, U.S. Army, Commanding

16 July 1944
To: Commanding General, First U.S. Army, A.P.O. 230

1. Approved.
2. General Williams has been directed to report to your headquarters, there being no appropriate assignment for him in the VIII Corps.
3. I do not know General Williams well, however, the fact that the 90th Division has not come up to expectations in combat is common knowledge. The Division Commander who brought the division to France has been relieved. I believe that new life and an improved attitude in the division can be developed by the assignment of a man as Assistant Division Commander who has proven himself in combat in this war, and who has had no relations with the division in the past.

Troy H. Middleton
Major General, U.S. Army, Commanding

Sam was not surprised, and after quickly reading the letter, he did not protest to Middleton, nor did Middleton seem to want to discuss the letter. He had put on his teaching mask and dismissed Sam as he would have a failed ROTC cadet during the early 1930s when he was a professor of military science and tactics at Louisiana State University.

This letter of July 14th was not a strong letter. It recognized Sam's immediate response in following Landrum's orders. Landrum, however, asked for a quieter and more docile brigadier general to be assigned as the Ninetieth assistant division commander. As Sam read the letter, he recalled his heated, ill-mannered harangue at Landrum, which he had ended by asking for his reassignment. Sam considered the letter a favorable response to his request. Middleton's comments and approval were direct, for he did not know Sam.

Sam knew that Landrum's letter could have an adverse effect on his career. He thought a change of jobs was not in itself limiting, and whereas the move from the Ninetieth would be painful, he could not see being punished by Bradley. He confidently expected to be given a responsible position somewhere in the First U.S. Army operational area.

Sam did not apologize or make excuses to Middleton for his performance with the Ninetieth Infantry Division or the performance of the division itself. Of course, he did not see his long association with the Ninetieth as contributing to its recent shortcomings, and he had not been the only officer responsible for its training and, hence, supposed "training deficiencies." Lieutenant Colonel Stilwell had been with the Ninetieth from the day of its activation in March of 1942 and had assumed staff responsibility for training when the division had moved to the California Desert Training Center. Major General Terrell had commanded the division on its activation and had remained with it until January of 1944 when MacKelvie arrived. Furthermore, others had played a pertinent role in the training of the infantry—the nine battalion commanders and the three regimental commanders. Sam knew that the division had successfully completed all of the requirements to qualify it for overseas service. Had the Ninetieth been found deficient in individual technical training or unit training, corrective measures would have been taken before its departure for England. This had not been the case; the Ninetieth had never been red-tagged for training deficiencies.[1]

Sam left Middleton's office and began the short trip to Bradley's headquarters to report to Maj. Gen. William B. Kean, chief of staff, First Army. Kean advised him that the paperwork on his case had not yet been received, nor was General Bradley present. He directed Sam to the headquarters' visitor area to await Bradley's return.

Two days later, on July 18th, a well-rested Sam asked to see Kean, and he was given a copy of the following recasting of Landrum's original letter seeking Sam's reassignment:

15 July 1944
Subject: Assistant Division Commander
To: Commanding General, VIII Corps, A.P.O 308, U.S. Army.

1. I request that an officer of combat experience in this war, preferably in this theater, be assigned as Assistant Division commander of this Division and that the present Assistant Division Commander Brigadier General Samuel T. Williams, 08472, U.S. Army (Inf), be relieved.

2. The relief of General Williams is requested on the following grounds:

a. He is not calm of temper, is excitable and these traits needlessly affect those with whom he deals.

b. His manner of speech is pessimistic and has caused me to lose confidence in the accuracy of his reports.

c. General Williams is not always discreet nor temperate of speech. On at least one occasion his unofficial conversation with an adjutant division commander caused doubt in the latter's mind as to the capacity of this division to attain its objective. This was at a time when the division was attaining its objective and was actually ahead of the adjacent division.

d. His first impulse is to adopt a defensive attitude when deficiencies in training have been brought to his attention by the undersigned, although he later readily admitted the existence of the deficiencies.

e. His intimate association with this division during its training period makes it difficult for him to assist in the remedying of training deficiencies that must be promptly detected and rapidly eliminated. General Williams has been the Assistant Division Commander of this division since 9 February 1943. From 24 November to 11 December 1943 he actually commanded the division while participating in maneuver training at the Desert Training Center.

f. I have lost confidence in this officer's capacity to give the help and assistance required of an assistant division commander under the conditions now existing. I believe that for the good of the division he should be removed from this division. I believe that new life and an improved attitude in the division can be furthered by the assignment of an officer as assistant division commander who has proven himself in combat in this war and who has had no relations with this division in the past.

3. I recommend that this officer be reduced to his permanent grade and temporarily appointed to the grade of colonel. This officer's energy and background justifies the assumption that useful employment in the grade of colonel can be found for him.

4. I consider this officer qualified to perform administrative duties in the grade of colonel or to command troops or installations other than in combat. His age alone precludes a prognosis of successful sustained command of combat troops in action.

5. Nothing in this letter should be construed as a reflection upon General Williams' honesty of purpose, his demonstrated personal bravery or his energy.

E. M. Landrum, Major General, U.S. Army, Commanding

18 July 1944
To: Commanding General, First U.S. Army, A.P.O. 230

1. Approved.

2. My observation and investigation of the Ninetieth Division leads me to believe that the infantry of the division was not as well trained for combat as one should reasonably expect. My limited observation of Brigadier General Williams has caused me to form the opinion that he is not an inspiring personality. My conversation with him leads me to believe that all was not well in the division during its training in the United States and after its arrival in England.

3. The division commander who brought this division to France was relieved while the division was serving in the VII Corps. I believe a further step toward lifting the division to its proper place as a reasonably good combat organization would be to replace General Williams with an officer of proven combat experience and one who has not been associated with the ups and downs of the division in the past.

4. Since I would not be willing to accept General Williams as an assistant division commander in another organization, I believe he should be returned to his temporary grade of colonel and be given an appropriate assignment other than with troops in combat.

Troy H. Middleton, Major General, U.S. Army, Commanding

To say that the letter dated July 15th shocked Sam is to express an understatement. It stunned and overwhelmed him, causing him a blow which, despite his future success and military honors, he would never forget. It was a devastating and crippling injury that pierced him to the core of his character. Middleton's endorsement was particularly disturbing to Sam because Middleton did not know him and had said so in his previous letter. Before he could say anything in rebuttal to Kean, he was told to report to General Bradley.

In Bradley's presence he recovered somewhat, but the forceful assistant division commander of the Ninetieth was less than confident. Without time to prepare, he tried to justify the division's poor showing and to indict Landrum for divisional mishaps. In the one-hour meeting with Bradley, Sam fumbled and lost the ball. Bradley dismissed him with the assurance that the matter would be further investigated before a final decision was made. Once again, Sam was told to return to his tent and wait.

Wait he did, until July 28th—which became for him ten days of self-judgment, hours of savage thoughts against Middleton (curiously, he did not feel betrayed by Landrum; he felt only anger), a growing uneasiness about his future, and a pulsating loss of confidence in his superiors who could not stand the exhausting demands of infantry battle. He reviewed in his mind the incompetence commanders such as MacKelvie and Landrum had shown faced with a strong German defense among the baffling hedgerows and weakening infantry morale. It had been true that the Ninetieth had been totally unprepared to fight in the *bocage* country, but Eisenhower, Bradley, and their staffs had made no efforts to anticipate the Germans' masterful hedgerow defenses and to condition the troops to face them. Sam also remembered the replacements for soldiers killed or wounded that had begun to arrive shortly after June 6th and which would equal one hundred percent of the enlisted strength of the division. Officer replacements had totaled more than 150 percent of the authorized infantry officers of the three regiments. Sam wondered how he could be held responsible for the training of replacements, who came from army infantry replacement centers as well as from many other sources to replenish the lost officers.

Kean called Sam on July 28th and handed him a letter, addressed to the G1 of Eisenhower's staff. Sam was charged to deliver his own sentence, as recommended by Bradley, to Eisenhower in London.

On arriving in London, Sam immediately reported to the G1 and was told to await instructions. The wait was not as unpleasant as had been the ten-day stay at Bradley's headquarters, nor was he surprised when he discovered that Landrum had been relieved and also was billeted in London. Sam made arrangements to meet with him.

Sam managed to restrain himself and temper his anger with Landrum when they met on August 3rd. He coolly asked Landrum for his reason in recommending that he be reduced. According to Sam, Landrum answered, "The reason I requested your *reduction,* after your departure from the division, was because they sent my letter back to me three times. It was an ultimatum. They said the only way I could effect your transfer was to ask for your reduction."[2] When Sam asked him for a written statement along these lines, Landrum declined, saying he could not reopen the case.

Later that day, Sam went to see the chief of staff, Gen. Walter B. Smith. After his quiet confrontation with Landrum, Sam had written a memorandum in which he told General Smith of his conversation with Landrum. He hoped that Landrum's comments would have a favorable influence on Eisenhower's decision, particularly with regard to his recommended reduction. Smith was absent, but Sam talked to a senior G1 officer about his situation and asked that Smith be advised that he would, if reduced, prefer to be returned to the United States so that he could land a job with some combat unit scheduled for assignment in Europe and that he would appreciate being assigned to Terrell's XXII Corps in any available duty space.

While in the G1 section, Sam was shown General Bradley's remarks, which were attached to Landrum's letter of July 15th. Bradley had approved the recommendations of Landrum and Middleton and added in his endorsement:

Brigadier General Williams was relieved from the division about ten days ago but has been held at this headquarters until the matter could be looked into. An informal investigation now has been made and it appears that General Williams has been very disappointed on two occasions by not being given command of the Ninetieth Division when the former commanders were relieved. He has let this affect his loyalty and spirit of cooperation with the new division commanders. It is considered unfortunate that his disappointment in not succeeding to command on these two occasions has thus influenced his usefulness because he is a hard worker and personally a very brave man.

Since he cannot be used for the purpose for which he was promoted, I recommend that he be reduced to his permanent grade then promoted to the temporary grade of Colonel and be given another chance to prove his usefulness.

Sam remained silent and merely shook his head in disbelief. Now his "loyalty and spirit of cooperation" were being questioned. In October of 1944, Sam would write to a captain friend about this and other accusations:

My contention was that my loyalty came first to you and other junior officers and soldiers in the outfit, the men who were slugging it out and to the Army of the U.S. and not to some dug-out Nell that never got forward to see what was what. To make a long disagreeable story short, that line of reasoning was judged by others to be wrong and I was disciplined.

Frankly, I still stand by my guns, cost what it may. For some reason I've never learned to kick a bunch of juniors in the balls just to hear them scream. . . .

It took me some time to piece the thing together but this seems to be the dope. Ted Roosevelt was slated to take over the division the day he died. Landrum had got word of this and was figuring desperately how he could hang on. As I had sounded off in no uncertain terms about what I considered boners that had been pulled topside, he attempted to convince others his difficulty in handling his job was my fault. Specifically that I sided with the troops against him and that he could not get me to make corrections. There was a lot of stuff about a lack of discipline and control in the Division which actually condemned him, in that he had had command for over 30 days.[3]

Unknown to Sam as he read Bradley's remarks in August, however, Eisenhower had already made the decision to recommend to Army Chief of Staff George Marshall that Sam be reduced for "unsatisfactory performance in combat." A message for General Marshall was dispatched to Washington at 1655 hours August 2nd. The message read:

> Relieved as Assistant Division Commander, Ninetieth Infantry Division, is Brigadier General SAMUEL T. WILLIAMS, 0-8472, for unsatisfactory performance in combat.
> Division, Corps, and Army Commanders' reports indicate that while General WILLIAMS is energetic and personally very brave, his performance has been such that he cannot be considered suitable for assignment as an Assistant Division Commander.
> Unless General WILLIAMS is especially desired by some branch or division of the War Department in his present grade, I request that you give me authority of the PRESIDENT to reduce him to his permanent grade of Lieutenant Colonel. I will immediately appoint him to the grade of Colonel, and can absorb him in this Theater.
> The report of the circumstances in connection with his relief will be forwarded to War Department promptly.

Two days later, on August 4th, General Smith honored Sam's request to be assigned to General Terrell's XXII Corps by recommending such action to General Marshall. This was a small victory for Sam. On 7 August 1944, Colonel Samuel T. Williams left London for Washington, D.C.

Two days after Col. Williams left England, Bradley wrote in a letter to Brig. Gen. Pleas B. Rogers, commander of the Central Base Section: "I was very sorry to have to send Sam Williams back. I had held on to him for several days until I could make a more thorough investigation. As you know, we have had a lot of trouble with that division. I don't know whose fault it is, but in order to try to solve it we have had to change a lot of the senior officers in the division."

Many officers of the Ninetieth were changed, but only one was reduced. Sam Williams took the full blow. Even so, he was not the only army officer ever to be "fired." The record is fraught with the names of general officers who were axed, busted, relieved, bounced. Why? Because of illness, personality conflicts, poor performance in combat, incompetency, or insubordination—all as perceived by fellow and senior officers. Sometimes, men were reduced with good reason; sometimes not. Lt. Gen. James M. Gavin wrote in his book *On to Berlin*, "I have a haunting memory that does not diminish with the passage of time of how unfairly and thoughtlessly we treated some of our senior officers [in World War II]."[4] Gavin's feelings could include Sam Williams, who was, as one man who witnessed his command in 1944 put it, "the wrong man." Gen. William E. DePuy said in 1979: "Landrum was not visible to the fighting troops. The man who was felt was 'Hanging Sam' [Williams]. And that is a tragic story because 'Hanging Sam' was fired. They got the wrong man. Williams was the ADC and he was with us all the time and was helpful and a very brave and powerful man as later everyone found out."[5]

"Hanging Sam" Williams, near Bad Tölz, Germany, 1948, with his German shepherd, Hoss.

Chapter 9 ☆ ☆ ☆ *Hanging Sam*

Lt. Col. Edwin Van Sutherland was the commanding officer of the Twenty-sixth Infantry Regiment with its headquarters located near Nuremberg. Sutherland later wrote of the arrival of a visitor:

It was in late January or early February 1946 when Colonel Williams arrived. My earliest memory of him is not an entirely pleasant one. Several of my officers, most of whom were well-decorated combat officers, had been with the "Big Red One" since Omaha beach. We were celebrating someone's birthday at our quarters in Erlangen, Germany, when we heard a heavy-handed knock on the front door. One of the younger officers opened it and invited the visitor to enter. It was bitter cold and snowing heavily outside. Col. Sam Williams stepped into the foyer and asked if we might have a room for his driver and one for himself.

Surprisingly, he was not wearing the insignia of a colonel on his field coat, yet upon entry he said, "I am Colonel Sam Williams."

As he stood in the doorway to the living room, he wiped the moisture from his glasses. As he did so his eyes moved for a short study to every officer present and it was obvious to me that he was weighing and evaluating each of them. You could feel the power of his presence. He demonstrated the calmest, strongest appearance I had ever observed in a senior officer.[1]

As Sam removed his coat, he directed a lieutenant to get his driver fed and to safeguard his vehicle. "He did not ask my permission to do so, nor did he need it," Sutherland noted.

Later that evening, Sam privately told Sutherland "I'm assuming command of the Twenty-sixth in two weeks, which will give you time to clear your books and prepare for your return to the States. Until you leave, I won't interfere with your operation or you, or your staff. I would like you to loan me a jeep and driver for a couple of weeks. Also, please let your unit commanders know that I'm in the area and will visit every company-sized unit without schedule or early announcement. I also intend to visit certain training areas in Bavaria, and I intend to recon the area and the locations of the regimental units with a view toward rebuilding them into a combat force."[2]

Shortly before meeting with Sutherland, Sam had played a key role in the deactivation of XXII Corps, having come to Bavaria from Czechoslovakia in mid-December 1945. He always viewed with pride his service with the XXII and its two commanding generals, Terrell and Harmon. Sam was especially grateful to Terrell because he had used his influence with the army ground forces commanding general, Lt. Gen. Ben Lear, to help him "get started" again.

When Sam had returned to Washington in August of 1944, he had met with General Lear. Before the meeting, he wrote a lengthy letter in which he explained, as he saw it, his reduction and relief by Bradley. Lear appeared to feel that Sam had been sacrificed unnecessarily by Bradley and Eisenhower. He offered

Sam a responsible position on his staff but was understanding when Sam asked that he be permitted to join General Terrell as the G3 of the XXII Corps located in Fort DuPont, Delaware.

Before going to Fort DuPont in September of 1944, Sam had given serious thought to his future. It looked bleak. Landrum's recommendation to have him reduced was a painful blow, but not a fatal one. The reduction had seriously damaged his reputation among his peers, and the untrue implication of Eisenhower's words—"unsatisfactory performance in combat"—was devastating to him. He reviewed his years of service and performance and found them favorable. Yes, he was tactless and too often outspoken, but to his knowledge, no soldier or officer had ever been injured or unfairly treated because of his bluntness.

Sam thought that perhaps he had made a serious blunder by not having served on the War Department general staff after completing the Army War College. Had he done so, Bradley and Eisenhower may have shown him some compassion, just as they had when MacKelvie was relieved. He felt rage because of Middleton's action, knowing that Middleton had admitted that he "did not know Williams" well. Sam wondered if perhaps a tour of ROTC during the early years might have led to an acquaintance with Middleton that might have softened his recommendation to Bradley.

Sam was aware too that his formal education did not include a university degree, but it was too late for him to correct that, and it had not been a consideration in his reduction anyway.

Sam had reported to Terrell on 13 September 1944. He continued his self-study throughout the months he was with the XXII. He came to the conclusion that it would take hard work and lady luck to help him retrieve his star, but he became fiercely determined to do so. He envisaged a need for new conflicts and a fresh image for himself. The first—a war—was certain to happen again, perhaps during his remaining active duty days, and the second—the image—he could devise.

Two months later, Sam was back in the European theater of operations with the corps. General Terrell did not accompany the XXII, having been relieved and sent to command a replacement training center in Louisiana. His age was a factor in his relief because Eisenhower wanted to have spaces to promote combat-experienced division commanders to lieutenant general. It was with this intention in mind that Eisenhower selected Maj. Gen. E.N. Harmon, a great commander of World War II's armored divisions, to become the commanding general of the XXII Corps.

Harmon picked up the corps in France in a location not far from where he had participated in the Battle of the Bulge. The corps officers did not please him, and he fired several and inserted in their places those he had observed in his divisions—the First, Second, and the Third Armored Divisions. Col. Sam Williams was advanced to the corps chief of staff where he remained until the corps was deactivated. For sixteen months, he was in a position that called for a brigadier general, but the star did not return.

Shortly after Harmon took command, the XXII was moved to the vicinity of the Rhine River where it became a major element of the Fifteenth Army, which, with its five divisions, created a thirty-mile defensive front on the banks of the Rhine. From Düsseldorf to the city of Cologne, the XXII awaited orders to attack, but the order never came. Bradley was closing a ring of steel around the Ruhr valley with the soldiers of the First and Ninth Armies. The XXII Corps was the base or fulcrum from which the last major attack by Americans in Europe during World War II would be launched.

Sam regretted that the XXII did not have the opportunity to demonstrate its combat readiness. But he was not aware that he would soon face huge problems that were, in analysis, far greater than any he had prepared himself to face in war. Massive, unrelated populations of humanity would confront the XXII commander and his staff. In the Rhineland alone, an area of farming and abundance in normal years, 600,000 hungry, sick, debilitated, exhausted people of every nationality and creed looked to the U.S. Army and the XXII Corps for a bite of food. It was a staggering challenge to Harmon, who was a great battle leader but also a compassionate person. His quick study of the problem overwhelmed him, but he was certain he could bring order out of the chaos of war. He recognized that the defeated Germans had no government; that the displaced people had nothing at all; that the escaped prisoners of war of diverse nationalities were given to revenge, murder, and mayhem; and that the bomb-scarred children, along with the seemingly endless, aimless elderly, were pleading for help, food, clothing, medical treatment, and attention.

Sam suggested categorizing the war victims. The wanderers were collected as humanely as possible and placed in camps organized by nationality. Placing them once again behind barbed wire under guard appeared to be a cruel solution; however, it allowed them to be quickly identified, permitted the isolation of criminals, and facilitated the immediate medical treatment for the sick and injured. It was a distasteful task. Sam Williams was happy when he received an order that directed the XXII to relieve the V Corps in Pilsen, Czechoslovakia. There, new encounters would arise because the Russians were occupying one-half of the country.

Sam made good use of his time in Czechoslovakia, studying the Russian Army and its soldiers. Later, during the Nuremberg Trials and in the beginning stages of the Russian-launched Berlin Blockade, he would apply what he had learned.

Eventually, the XXII received a warning order from the Third Army, its parent unit, that it was to prepare for redeployment from Czechoslovakia. It was to clear the country by 30 November 1945, the same day the Russians would also depart. Unlike the Americans, however, the Russians would leave behind their Moscow-trained cadres, which would seize control of the little country a few years later. General Harmon left for another assignment after making his farewell speech in Pilsen's city square. Sam managed the XXII's withdrawal from Czechoslovakia with little difficulty. He also made good use of his meetings with the Third Army by asking for, and being given, a troop command. One factor that influenced Third Army assignment officials was the numerical rating Sam received from General

Harmon: a perfect 7.0, the highest score possible and one rarely earned by even the most outstanding officers. Harmon recognized that Colonel Williams was of the caliber the U.S. Army needed for leadership in the post-war army in stricken Germany. He was selected to command the Twenty-sixth Infantry Regiment located in Nuremberg.

In June of 1944, the victorious U.S. Army had fielded a combat force of sixty-one divisions in Europe, supported by 1.6 million medics, quartermasters, engineers, truckers, armorers, communicators, and others. On VE Day, they all cleared their weapons, folded their maps, and, as conquerors have always done, began to look for other action. They were young men who had passed the test of combat, saddened by the loss of friends but energized by the glow of health and youth. They were the victors and ready to take advantage of the opportunities to be found in occupied Germany. George Bernard Shaw recognized the victor's disposition when he wrote "When the military man approaches, the world locks up its spoons and packs off its womenkind." The young men—officers and soldiers alike—too often were unrestrained by Eisenhower's nonfraternization policy. To carouse with scant possibility of correction, to imbibe to excess without having to respond to the bugle or the bark of a sergeant, to consort with statuesque German fräuleins, was proper reward for the combat veteran. But when they were sober, alert, and controlled, the occupation force did good work.

Public pressure to "bring the boys home" resulted in the departure of more than 3 million troops by January of 1946, which meant that a combat-ready force of regimental strength among those remaining could not be found. By the end of December, 1945, the U.S. Army was a depleted, stricken element, 93,000 soldiers short of its authorization. When Sam became commander of the Twenty-sixth Infantry Regiment—or the Blue Spaders—the First Infantry Division and the newly formed cavalry force, the U.S. Constabulary, were the remaining elements of a once magnificent force of five U.S. armies.

After the XXII was deactivated, Sam had returned to Fort

Worth, Texas, where he spent Christmas of 1945 with Jewell. Returning to Germany in early February, he became acquainted with the soldiers, officers, and condition of the Twenty-sixth Infantry Regiment.

During the next two weeks, Sam visited the headquarters of the Big Red One where he was oriented on the mission of the First Division and the Twenty-sixth Infantry Regiment. He had lengthy discussions with the division staff and spent several hours with Brig. Gen. Clift Andrus, the division's commanding general. Sam knew Andrus slightly because Andrus had built a reputation for his keen use of artillery as the First Division's artillery commander. Sam told Andrus that he was proud to be named the regimental commander of the Blue Spaders, and Andrus saw in Sam an "Old Army" officer—disciplined, confident, loyal, and strong. Sam also advised Andrus that the regiment's condition was less than satisfactory and that the unit had serious morale and discipline problems. "Its efficiency can be recovered," Sam said, "but it will call for extraordinary efforts and unusual techniques of leadership to restore the reputation and esprit de corps that it once had. I will begin immediately."[3]

Sam particularly felt that the regiment had a serious command problem. Not a single company of any of the rifle battalions was commanded by a captain, and most companies were short of authorized officers and soldiers of all ranks and skills. Two battalions were headed by acting commanders in the grade of major, and the other was commanded by a well-known lieutenant colonel—John T. Corley—who was on temporary duty in the States. Sam also informed Andrus that the regimental vehicles were in terrible shape, radios did not work and were not being maintained, and weapons were deadlined or missing. Sam did not suggest that Andrus or his staff was failing to fulfill the obligations of command, but he did say that an immediate change was going to be made in the Blue Spaders, and he asked for Andrus' support.

Another factor that Sam believed contributed to the Blue Spaders' ineffectiveness and lack of discipline was that the units were located far from their parent headquarters. The First Battalion was in Ludwigsburg, the Second in Munich, and the Third in the Fürth-Nuremberg area. Little military training was possible because the soldiers were cutting and hauling firewood for the sick, transporting displaced people, and operating mess halls for the functionaries of the War Crimes Trials, the press, and visitors, as well as remnants of those war followers who accumulate after victory. Prostitution thrived, and venereal disease was rampant. A cigarette economy prevailed and much of the military scrip that the army was trying to install found its way into the hands and wallets of the Germans and the displaced people. The black market was widespread and largely unchecked despite efforts of the occupation administrators to control it. Loose living, carousing by officers and soldiers, looting, murder, rape, assault, and drunken driving were commonplace. The unfettered American soldier was unwilling to accept the rigors of daily discipline and army control.

Sam decided that this would be the time to begin to create the new image he had envisioned two years earlier. Toward that end, he decided to revive his dormant nickname: "Hanging Sam" Williams. Sam had not coined his own nickname as had "Blood and Guts" Patton. Rather, "Hanging Sam" had come about because of Sam's inherent impatience, exemplified by a particular incident: He was a member of a general court-martial in which the accused was being tried for the rape and murder of a little girl. The prosecutor and the counsel for the defense waged a seemingly endless duel by offering the testimony of a parade of psychiatrists, each attempting to influence the members of the court by offering "expert" opinions as to the accused's sanity or lack of it. Their testimony became repetitious and tiring to Sam, so interrupting one of them he said, "I've heard enough! Let's hang the sonovabitch!"

Not all approved of Sam's moniker. Brig. Gen. Francis A. Woolfley, who had known Sam as a student at Leavenworth and the War College in the 1930s wrote: "I treasure the memory of my long friendship with Sam Williams and I resent the title of

Hanging Sam for . . . this title does not reflect his character. He was forthright and aggressive but a considerate individual with a deep loyalty to his subordinates and [he] was particularly dedicated to the welfare of all in his command."[4]

But unknown to General Woolfley, the Sam Williams of the mid-1940s was a changed man from that of the 1930s, and his later leadership techniques, which he consciously altered, reflected a different Sam Williams to the end of his days in 1984. "Hanging Sam" did, quite positively, reflect a studied transformation in Sam's personality and habits.

Sam decided that this nickname would serve a purpose in his plans for the Blue Spaders. He knew that soldiers identified particularly well with leaders who had a slick moniker or motto, such as "Iron Mike" O'Daniels, "Stonewall" Jackson, "Black Jack" Pershing, and "Blood and Guts" Patton. The Blue Spaders definitely needed a personal commander and unit identification, which had been lost, and new respect for authority, which also had been eroded.

So it was "Hanging Sam" Williams who took command of the Blue Spaders in February of 1946.[5]

Hanging Sam, at the age of forty-nine, was physically impressive. His military posture and soldierly carriage, although not stiff, nonetheless testified to the profession he chose to follow. With shoulders centered and level, his hips carried his upper body with an evenness that showed the strength and power of an infantry commander. His right arm was ever ready to return a salute, which he always rendered smartly. Invariably, he carried a riding crop, a habit he had developed during his polo-playing days but had not practiced during his service with the Ninetieth.

His clothing was impeccable, neat and pressed no matter the weather conditions, which was disconcerting to staff officers and subordinates who accompanied Sam in the field and felt filthy and unkempt next to him. Frequently, he grew a mustache, which he kept fairly large but always well-trimmed. His hair, however, was usually in disarray for it bristled even moments after stepping out of a barber's chair. His lined face presented a stern, tight-lipped appearance that was heightened by deep-set eyes that always signaled his mood of the moment.

The most serious matter facing Hanging Sam when he took over the Blue Spaders was the lack of discipline throughout the regiment. The use of company punishment for minor offenses was seldom applied, largely because of the inexperience of the company commanders. Sam concluded that far too many Blue Spaders were being court-martialed, which resulted in lost manpower because of pretrial confinement. To lower the high court-martial rate, Sam appointed a Courts-Martial Officer—a lieutenant with some legal training who demonstrated greater talent for judicial work than for the art of platoon leadership. This officer was required to handle all matters relating to boards and courts and to instruct members of the command as to the use of military justice.

During Sam's visits to units, he discovered that many first sergeants and company commanders did not know the number of soldiers they were assigned, were unfamiliar with their exact location, and were unable to account for them. Sam directed that rosters be forwarded immediately to the Twenty-sixth Infantry personnel officer that gave each soldier's name, serial number, rank, location, and immediate officer supervisor. According to the personnel officer and the regimental S1, the strength of the regiment was "appreciably increased" after all the rosters had been studied.[6]

Sam also investigated the high incidence of vehicle accidents within his command. The regimental motor officer, Lt. Wilson Snyder, was directed to requalify every driver of the unit vehicles, to tighten procedures that authorized dispatch, and to recall vehicles at night with assembly in a controlled setting. Sam also ordered Snyder to establish roadside vehicle inspection teams in order to quickly determine a vehicle's serviceability. Faulty vehicles would be impounded, and Sam would be advised promptly. To gain the vehicle's release, the company commander would have to appear before Hanging Sam and be "counseled," which for most commanders was a shattering experience.

Another practice Sam started was required weekly reveille and retreat formations with all personnel present. Sam would hold the soldiers in formation and question them as to their jobs, training, and backgrounds. A soldier was often asked to tell Sam the name of his platoon sergeant and the name of his company commander. Hell would be coming for any young commander if Sam discovered two or more soldiers who did not know the name of their "Old Man." Sam would be amused if, when asking a soldier to give him the name of his rifle company commander, the soldier would blurt "Hanging Sam Williams, sir."

Still another requirement Hanging Sam placed on the unit commanders was to revise the soldiers' monthly payment procedures. When Sam arrived, the lowest ranking commissioned officer paid the company members, who reported to him at company headquarters. But Sam ordered the commanders to pay their soldiers where they lived and worked. In this way, the commanders became better acquainted with their soldiers and frequently discovered adverse situations that they then could correct before Sam heard of them.

Yet the most unique innovation Hanging Sam installed was a regimental-wide information service for his personal use. Few knew of this confidential service because he did not publicize it even to his most intimate associates. The information network was manned by key regimental noncommissioned officers, such as the personnel sergeant, the medical dispensary senior sergeant, the officer club assistant, the provost sergeant, the S2 sergeant, and the finance sergeant. Each was unaware that the network existed. Simply stated, the structure called for Sam to be advised directly and quietly by the sergeants if anything unusual or untoward occurred within the framework of their responsibility. Thus, Sam learned of such things as the abuse of a dependent wife by her officer husband and a huge gambling debt owed an enlisted man by an officer. He also was advised of a chaplain's heavy drinking and of an adulterous affair involving a sergeant and an officer's spouse.

Before bringing a noncommissioned officer into this infrastructure, Sam explained to the man his duty. He was adamant in this orientation that the sergeant did not think of himself as an informer, tattle-tale, or spy. In Sam's view, the participant was giving Sam early information about a condition or situation that Sam would eventually discover anyway.

Thus, battalion commanders might be astonished when, for example, Sam would telephone them before breakfast and inquire what they were going to do about an officer from their battalion who was arrested by the MPs for being found in an off-limits whorehouse.

Sam also began some basic training, emphasizing the fundamentals of soldiering and bringing noticeable corrections in military courtesy, discipline, military security, administrative procedures, and supply conservation. Hanging Sam was severe with any officer whom he discovered was failing to conduct required instruction.

This modest start gave momentum to what became the finest trained regiment in the Big Red One. During a visit to the Blue Spaders, the secretary of the army, Kenneth Royal, publicly said, "The review of the Twenty-sixth Infantry Regimental Combat Team exhibited a readiness which exceeds anything I have yet seen, even in training camps at home during the war."[7]

Hanging Sam's tour with the Blue Spaders continued until April of 1947. During those fourteen months, he was appointed acting commanding general of the First Infantry Division after the departure of General Andrus and before the arrival of his friend from Leavenworth days, Maj. Gen. Frank W. Milburn. He also served another thirty days as acting assistant division commander. During any absences from the Spaders, Sam did not relinquish command or remain remote from what was happening in the regiment.

Against his vocal and written objections, Sam was returned home for an assignment in the Pentagon with the Civil Affairs Division, a segment of the War Department's Special Staff. He was uncomfortable in this position, which entailed hiring civilians for textile and railroad offices within the German government. But his fortune improved after he discovered that Gen. Lucius Clay, the U.S. military governor in Germany, was visiting Pentagon officials. Sam went to see him and soon received orders to return to Germany as the executive officer of the First Military District, a part of the military government operation. Jewell accompanied him to this assignment, but not two months later, he returned to the Twenty-sixth Infantry Regiment.

Hanging Sam was back. It was January of 1948.

The mission of the Blue Spaders was to be ready on twenty-four hours' notice for commitment anywhere in any part of the European Command. But once again, Hanging Sam made a detailed visit to his units and came away discouraged. He was skeptical about his regiment's capability to accomplish its mission, but he knew how to correct its limitations—training, training, and more training.

After coordination with and guidance from his superiors, Sam intensified the training and was influential in having the entire regiment stationed in Bamberg, Germany, where he began full-time small-arms and crew-served weapons training. Sam also created special schools for intensive instruction, covering every means of communication used by his regiment. He was ruthless with those officers he found to be lackadaisical or unwilling to accept the seriousness of the situation.

He enhanced training by eliminating every factor that detracted from it. Normal after-duty hours were dedicated to athletics, but practice was not permitted during normal duty hours. Cooks and bakers found themselves actively engaged with cleaning kettles at the same time they polished M-1's; clerks typed morning reports as they prepared to man a machine gun. There was no compromise; training was the sole purpose of the Blue Spaders.

But Sam wanted a perfect training ground. When he had visited his units in February of 1946, he had taken time to reconnoiter a former German training ground called Grafenwöhr. The area had been a major training post for the Germans for years; during the Hitler years, it had been developed into the Wermacht's finest training facility. Sam found it to be adaptable to his training and maneuver needs and enthusiastically recommended the area to Andrus and others.

The Twenty-sixth Infantry Regiment was the first army unit to occupy and train in Grafenwöhr. Sam planned and helped create a canvas billeting area that became known as Tent City. Later, intensive construction work was done. Rough, tar-papered headquarters buildings were built as well as other buildings essential to the operation, such as dispensaries, communication centers, and storage facilities. The soldiers' living situation improved somewhat after wooden floors were placed under the tents, and ten-holer company latrines were started to the lee side of the mess halls.

The entire regiment eventually was assembled at Grafenwöhr, with living tents and supply tents on the south side of the regimental road and wooden frame kitchens and mess halls on the other. It was crude, rough, and unaesthetic, but it was functional. From his command standpoint, Sam found it to be beautiful; now he had his Blue Spaders assembled in one location and in an area that gave him greater control and offered the best training areas and ranges in all of Europe—Grafenwöhr.

☆　☆　☆

In the Bavarian dawn mist, two American infantrymen, one carrying the folded national colors, emerge from the regimental headquarters building in the faint early-morning light. They are accompanied by two unusually tall armed escorts. Stopping them for a moment in front of the Blue Spader flag pole, the color guard sergeant orders:

"Post—MARCH!"

The color guard moves quietly to positions near the pole. Two of them affix the halyards to the flag's grommets. Nearby, the regimental duty officer watches as the Drum and Bugle Corps is positioned. Without order, a bugler sounds First Call.

It is time for reveille to be sounded for the soldiers of the Twenty-sixth Infantry Regiment in Grafenwöhr, Germany.

The duty officer scans his watch and calmly says, "Sound reveille and present arms." The color guard sergeant directs, "Sound reveille," and then orders, "Present ARMS." As he does so, a morning gun is fired, its echoes reverberating across the training area. At the same time, a bugler blows the service melody of reveille.

When the bugle call ends, the color guard sergeant orders, "Port ARMS; forward MARCH."

With that, the color guard moves toward the Twenty-sixth Infantry Regiment headquarters. The Drum and Bugle Corps also marches off to a drummer's tap, tap. When they reach the Blue Spade Road, the formation halts and faces east.

Just beyond the ring of the reveille performers, Colonel Sam Williams lowers his hand from salute and moves to the regimental road. When he arrives, the Drum and Bugle Corps moves to the east, stepping off in a lively fashion to the notes of "Dixie."

"Come on Hoss. Let's take a walk," Sam says to his dog. Hoss follows, keeping a trained distance to Sam's left and rear.

The duty officer returns to his station and tells a corporal, "Call Able Company and tell them Hanging Sam is on his way. Tell them to pass it on."

☆   ☆   ☆

Hanging Sam's morning walks offered him the opportunity to talk informally with his soldiers and officers. He used the time to examine property books of various companies and inspect weapons. Frequently, he would have breakfast in one of the twenty mess halls, during which he would observe the condition of the Spaders' uniforms, as well as their personal appearances. These excursions through the regiment were closely watched by the unit commanders who, after Sam's departure, would telephone others and tell them what was "on Sam's mind this morning."

Hanging Sam served with the First Infantry Division for more than forty-four months, usually as commanding officer of the Twenty-sixth Infantry Regiment. Throughout those duty days, he was a strong advocate of competition among his own units, and he supported division competition as well. His Spaders presented him with many winning plaques and trophies of victory. He was especially proud of those victories that showed superiority in matters military. Weapons firing, close-order drill, best-drilled soldier, and crew drill competitions pleased him the most.

As the Twenty-sixth Infantry improved, it became recognized as the best-trained and combat-ready regiment in Europe. It had maneuvered against the Sixteenth, Eighteenth, and the Constabulary in several exercises and had been found "razor sharp." It was obvious that the regiment might soon be given an operational mission with Berlin as its objective.

The Russians, jubilant with the seizure of Czechoslovakia, looked elsewhere for places to conquer, and it appeared that the next incursion would be to annex all of Berlin. They were belligerent and restricted U.S. access to West Berlin by road. On 30 March 1948, the Soviets announced that henceforth all ground transport and vessels en route to Berlin through the Soviet Occupation Zone would be subject to search, thus delaying and hindering resupply of American forces and the entire civilian population.

General Milburn's office contacted Sam in early April and advised him that Milburn would soon arrive at the small airstrip in Grafenwöhr. Sam met him and the two drove to an isolated range where they could talk. "Shrimp" Milburn told Sam of the seriousness of the situation in Berlin. General Clay expected to break the blockade with the Twenty-sixth Infantry as the central element of a reinforced Twenty-sixth Regimental Combat Team. Milburn produced a map that they used to closely study the autobahn that went from Hoff, through the Russian Zone, and on to Berlin. Milburn told Sam that General Clay wanted to beef up the Twenty-sixth until it represented an international force of battalion-sized units from France, Britain, and perhaps Belgium. Sam declined such large units and accepted a British company he knew could fight, and, hesitantly, a company of French. "None of them meets our standards," Sam said. He saw no need to impede his operation with battalion sized tea-breaks, and he disliked the French military unless they were equipped and trained by the French Foreign Legion. Sam's breakthrough force eventually was strengthened with the addition of the First Division tanks, engineers, and a logistical tail, together with one company of French and a company of British infantry.

The successful Berlin Airlift overrode the planned use of the Twenty-sixth Infantry to influence the Berlin Blockade. Sam later joined others in the speculative debate as to the outcome of an attempt to break the blockade if he had been ordered to move. Sam felt that they could go through without firing a shot. However, Sam asked Milburn to give him written orders anyway. "Knowing the State Department's love for Russians," Sam is reported to have said, "I do not want this busted general to be court-martialed for the unauthorized killing of a communist."

Hanging Sam did not allow the Berlin Blockade interlude to interfere with his preparation of the Blue Spaders for combat. Retraining was necessary and vital to the maintenance and readiness of the command. Key regiment officers were selected for major staff roles at higher headquarters, and the ever-moving hand of time caused a continuous rotation of officers and enlisted leaders. Training was cycled to an annual basis which, in the Twenty-sixth, quickly helped solve personnel problems.

Field problems presented fresh challenges for commanders and their staffs. Wide-ranging maneuvers conducted throughout western Germany and involving combat forces located in Europe sharpened the capabilities. Operations and exercises—"Snowdrop," "Normal," "Showers," and "Harvest"—were increasingly realistic and demanding tests of the commanders, their staffs, and the troops. Reports from umpires, observers, and senior officers never found the Twenty-sixth Infantry deficient.

Hanging Sam Williams had raised the efficiency of the Blue Spaders to a peak of competency with confidence and stability of the highest order. In June of 1950, Colonel Williams returned to Fort Monroe, Virginia, to serve in the Operations and

Training Office of the Army Field Forces.

Maj. Gen. John E. Dahlquist, Headquarters First Infantry Division, in completing Colonel Williams' annual Efficiency Report (June 1950), commented:

> Colonel Williams is in excellent physical condition and displays splendid military bearing. His standards are the highest and he is extremely loyal in every way. His knowledge of administration, training and tactics is outstanding. I consider him the finest regimental commander I have ever known. His regiment has constantly been the best in the division in every endeavor. Colonel Williams should be promoted to Brigadier General because of his outstanding record and value to the Army.

The endorsing officer, Lt. Gen. Clarence R. Hubner, the commanding general, U.S. Army, Europe, wrote:

> I concur heartily with the comments and ratings of the rating officer and in addition add: that not only is this officer one of the finest commanders I have ever seen but he has great vision and foresight. The fact that he was relieved of his command and demoted from Brigadier General to grade of Colonel should not cause the Army to lose his services. I do recommend that he be promoted to Brigadier General at once and kept on assignments that have to do with commanding and leading our young American soldiers. I feel that a very great injustice has been done to this superb officer by not promoting him to General Officer rank.

Then, in an unusual departure from standard army procedures, General Dahlquist wrote to Army Chief of Staff Gen. J. Lawton Collins. His letter was dated 26 July 1950:

Dear General Collins:

> Colonel Sam T. Williams, 08472, who has commanded the 26th Infantry for the past three years, has just departed from the 1st Division for a new assignment with Army Field Forces.

Colonel Williams' service with the 1st Division has been so outstanding that I feel he should be called to your personal attention. In my opinion he is the ablest troop commander that has served under me. His regiment is by all odds the outstanding unit in Germany today, and that is due to him.

He is a splendid administrator, trainer and leader. Above all he is loyal to his commander. I feel that he is fully qualified for any staff or command position. He would make a first class division commander.

Sincerely,
John E. Dahlquist
Major General, U.S. Army, Commanding

(Next page) President Syngman Rhee awards the Gold Star Ulchi Medal to Gen. Samuel T. Williams, 1953. At one point during his Korean tour, Sam was placed in the South Korean army chain of command.

(Below) General Maxwell D. Taylor (left) with General Williams (right) in 1954 when Williams was commander of IX Corps.

(Above) Major General Williams, 1954.

Chapter 10 ☆ ☆ ☆ *A Star Returns*

The Williams' returned to the United States in June of 1950 by crossing the Atlantic aboard the MSTS *Goethals*. The voyage was Jewell's choice for she liked shipboard life and its routines. Sam, however, was not enchanted with the blue sky and the deep waters of the Atlantic because he did not know how to swim.

The soldiers aboard the stricken *Susan B. Anthony* in 1944 had been unaware of this. No doubt those soldiers who had so closely followed his orders to evacuate the *Anthony* would have been amused had they known. In 1918, Sam had been floated across the Meuse River during a river-crossing operation. He laid spread-eagle on a heavy house door, pistol in hand and under the watchful eyes of two swimming sergeants was steered to the opposite shore.

Sam felt that the time spent crossing the Atlantic was wasted, but he made the most of it by reading and reflecting on his career and his future. Once again, forces were on the move in other parts of the world, and Sam wanted to join them. On June 25th, a North Korean force of ten small infantry divisions had invaded South Korea. Even though it lacked naval and air power, it was a formidable attacker. The leadership of North Korea was, apparently, confident they could overrun South Korea with little effort and minimal losses.

The South Korean Army at that time was little more than a constabulary element of 95,000 ineffectives. It lacked the skill, equipment, and leadership necessary even to slow down the invaders. In three days, the North Korean communist army had captured South Korea's capital city and was occupying the north banks of the Han River.

The United Nations asked the United States to establish a command to fight the invaders. President Truman agreed to do so and selected Gen. Douglas MacArthur to lead it. The South Korean Army was soon placed under the colors of the U.S. Eighth Army, commanded by Lt. Gen. Walton H. Walker. As other United Nations Command (UNC) forces arrived in South Korea, they were assimilated into the Eighth Army.

By mid-August General Walker's army was compressed and cornered in southeastern Korea. Walker drew a circle on his map and said, "Here we will stand"; the stand area became known as the Pusan Perimeter.

When Sam and Jewell arrived in the States, Sam, in typical stormy fashion, stopped first at the Pentagon where he tried, without success, to have canceled the orders that instructed him to report to the Army Field Force Command (AFF) in Fort Monroe, Virginia. Eager to be where the fighting was, he wanted to be redirected to South Korea with assignment to any combat unit of the Eighth Army. The Department of the Army personnel staff was not persuaded, and Sam was told that his AFF assignment was a "stabilized" tour, meaning that three years of commanding a desk faced him. This was a better pill for Sam to swallow.

After a brief leave in Denton, Sam and Jewell arrived at Fort Monroe and moved into a forty-year-old duplex built for captains' occupancy at a cost, in 1910, of $26,662. Its location was a peaceful one for Jewell, with St. Mary's Star of the Sea Church opposite and the banks of the Chesapeake Bay but a minute's walk away. Sam also liked the quarters because from there he could walk to the on-post Chamberlain Hotel where he would join other AFF staff members for coffee and breakfast. The home was comfortable and well furnished after Sam gathered their belongings from Texas and Germany.

Before long, however, Sam began to display signs of discontent. He grumbled to Jewell about the endless flow of paper to his office, growled about his one hundred civilian employees, and talked of retiring. He watched the military situation closely by avidly reading classified reports and, at breakfast, the morning edition of the *Washington Post*. The entry of the Chinese into the conflict, followed by another retreat of the UNC forces to south of Seoul, caused him anguish. He yearned for another chance to disprove Eisenhower's haunting remark about his "unsatisfactory performance in combat" by leading Americans in combat. He was beginning to doubt he would ever again command troops in a wartime situation.

Jewell recognized her husband's restlessness as he began talking about their future. His mail soon became heavy with letters from cattle breeding associations and real estate dealers offering land for sale from Oregon to Texas. Her conversations with him seemed to lead to discussions about a little spread with a few Herefords, a couple of AKC pups, plus a thoroughbred stud and several brood mares. He talked of his health, which was good, and how he could handle a few acres.

Jewell mildly reminded Sam of his dream to regain his star and how the war in distant Korea might prove to be the critical factor in his selection for promotion. Her thinking prevailed, and Sam continued to serve as AFF G3 executive officer. His superior, Maj. Gen. M.B. Halsey, wrote in a January 1951 Efficiency Report that Sam was "an officer of mature judgment, with high appreciation of the commander's responsibility. A man

of action. Highly effective in organizing his work. Follows through."
Halsey felt that Sam would perform competently and dependably
as a major general. Gen. Mark Clark, AFF chief, noted that Sam
was one of the few highly outstanding officers he knew.

Much to his surprise, Colonel Samuel T. Williams was
promoted to brigadier general on Tuesday, 13 February 1951.
General Williams later wrote, "Probably everybody in the army
[was] as surprised as I [was]. I guess the powers that be decided
that I [had] had enough disciplinary action."[1] For seven years and
four months, Sam had looked forward to this day and the return
of his star. He had come back.

General Sam Williams continued to serve in the AFF as
deputy G3 because a successor to General Halsey had not been
nominated. His staff duties were heavy: he was responsible for
the supervision, direction, and coordination of the AFF Combined
Arms Division, the Schools Division, and the Civilian Compo-
nents Division. He also was required to visit installations as
necessary. One such inspection trip long remained in Sam's
memory.

Lt. Gen. Frank W. Milburn, AFF inspector of infantry,
asked Clark if he could borrow Sam for an inspection trip to the
European Command. Milburn was carrying out an inspection
and also had been directed by General Collins to investigate the
levels of certain critical weapons, equipment, and ammunition.
The strength of the U.S. Army after 1 July 1950 had increased
significantly. From 665,000 officers and men it rose to a peak of
more than 1.5 million by 30 March 1952. In addition to troop
deployments for the Korean conflict, four combat divisions and
various combat and combat-support units were deployed to the
U.S. Army, Europe, as part of the buildup of the NATO defense
shield. Milburn's crew was to report imbalances in order to
correct management errors.

For Sam, the return to Germany in September of 1951 was
a homecoming. He carried out the requirements and responsibilities of the inspection team but also found time to pay a visit to his
old unit—the Twenty-sixth Infantry Regiment Blue Spaders—
which was still garrisoned in Bamberg, Germany. While there, he

was asked to present the winner's plaque to the 1951 European Command baseball champions—a team from the Blue Spaders. He considered this an honor and said so, adding that he was "pleased to know the Spaders were continuing their winning tradition."[2]

During the flight back to Washington, Sam and Milburn talked at length about the Korean conflict. Milburn was knowledgeable about the fighting there, having commanded I Corps from 10 September 1950 until 18 July 1951. Sam learned much from these conversations, as he normally did when listening to senior officers whom he respected, not only for their rank, but most of all for their proven leadership ability.

Since November of 1951, the battlefront in Korea had been stabilized, but in May of 1952, the enemy became more aggressive, applying pressure across the entire Eighth Army front. Frequent enemy attempts to seize key points and terrain led to intense firefights.

After many earnest and serious appeals, Sam finally arrived in Korea in June of 1952. On June 17th, Brigadier General Williams took command of the Twenty-fifth Infantry Division, which once had been commanded during the early days of World War II by "Lightning Joe" Collins.

The principal organic regiments of the Twenty-fifth Division were the Fourteenth, the Twenty-seventh (the Wolfhounds), and the Thirty-fifth. Two additional units, the Fifth Infantry Regiment and the 555th Artillery, plus engineers, medical, and other service units, raised the strength of the division to more than 30,000, probably the heaviest in South Korea at that time.

Sam found the infantrymen in good shape, or they became so shortly after his arrival. Esprit de corps was high in the Wolfhounds and good in the other two regiments. He secretly admired the Wolfhounds because they reminded him of the Blue Spaders. It thrilled him that 390 soldiers from the Big Red One, most of whom were Blue Spaders, had volunteered to leave the relative comfort of Bamberg and come to fight with him and his Twenty-fifth Division in Korea during 1952 and 1953.

From the day he assumed command, Sam did those things

that he knew needed to be done, wanting to bring his division to peak efficiency within the shortest possible time. Surprisingly, to him, he found the division rated high, even when his pedantic management standards were applied. As usual, he visited every platoon in the division and talked to every company commander. He ate with them and watched them prepare for patrols and discovered that he had inherited a good division. In a letter written 22 September 1952 to Col. Granville A. Sharpe, he wrote of his division, "I'm beginning to collect some very good, outstanding soldiers in this Division from many sources. Except for the occupational hazard involved, I don't think you will regret your service here."

His daily routine reflected that which he had followed in the Ninetieth as assistant division commander. Up before dawn, Sam visited his communication center for any "just received" messages, then went to the G3 center where he would be briefed on activities that had occurred during the night. Breakfast was sometimes followed by a short staff meeting, and then he would be off to the field. First he would visit any unit that had experienced a night firefight or had conducted a successful, or even unsuccessful, patrol. Frequently, he would go to the supporting medical unit to present wounded soldiers with Purple Hearts and medals for valor. Using the daylight hours for contact with his men, he pursued administrative matters during the hours of darkness, sometimes after watching a cowboy movie if one were available. Maj. Gen. Charles G. Case remembered that Sam "loved movies . . . and particularly liked westerns. His serenity at these times was in marked contrast to his tempestuous tirades when someone was evasive or misleading or 'unprofessional' or just plain screwed up."[3]

Sam discovered that more than fifty percent of his line companies were commanded by lieutenants with fewer than two years of service and that battalion commanders were young. He wrote of his commanders:

> They usually run in their late 30s and need to because of the violent (to me) physical exertions they must go through to

climb these hills and get about their battalions. . . . The brutal facts are these: Battalion commanders are young, most company commanders are kids of 22–25 years of age. Regimental commanders run about 38. Assistant division commanders are about 40. It simply is not a question of how much a man knows, but, coupled with that, can he get up and down these hills day in and day out. (Letter to Lt. Col. A.V. Williams, 6 November 1952.)

But the youth and inexperience of some of his lieutenants also meant that Sam found himself doing things that he had last done in France in 1918. He wrote, "A general officer must recall those things he knew as a platoon leader and company commander. It's not unusual for me to employ correctly a machine gun in a defensive position and I frequently am required to demonstrate how to build a firing trench, or supervise the rebuilding of a poorly constructed one. I find that lieutenants and battalion commanders both need advice and assistance with their tasks." (Letter to Chaplain Herbert Evans, 4 January 1953.) In a letter to Col. George A. Clayton 23 September 1952, he elaborated on his early experiences in Korea and the soldiers he found there:

Things are going along here just as you might expect. . . . The enemy is more curious and has come to us occasionally which, incidentally, keeps us from having to go so far to find him. His "poor man's artillery" is rather accurate and, at times, none too pleasan . . . it is increasingly necessary for one to keep his eye on the next available shelter as one walks along. Personally, I find it more and more difficult to act indifferent and nonchalant about his incoming trash. Old age probably. It would be a disgrace to be crippled-up by these heathen bastards!

I'm learning considerable here, and more and more see the similarity between this current-position warfare and my experiences as a platoon and company commander in the early part of World War I.

One of the most important things I've learned is that our junior officers are taught to fight "perfect" units and not partially trained privates and NCOs. Also, that most of our officers, of all rank, need more detailed supervision than they did in World War I or II. Complacency is a dreadful disease and can cost like hell. No one seems to care too much about correcting minor omissions until someone gets hurt.

As always, Sam tackled every problem and faced new challenges and situations eagerly. For instance, a Turkish brigade of about 5,000 soldiers was attached to Sam's division when he took command. Gen. Mark Clark wrote in his book *From the Danube to the Yalu* that Sam had some difficulties with the Turks.[4] In particular, they were reluctant to use the provided bathing facilities in the Twenty-fifth Infantry Division, and consequently, many exuded a less-than-desirable body odor. Sam received complaints from American soldiers. When he discovered that Turks do not disrobe in public, he solved the problem by providing them with private bathing facilities.

Clark also wrote:

> Williams had other problems with the Turks. He had trouble getting them to begin fighting on time in operations in which coordination between units was essential. Each time he complained about the Turks lagging he was told by the Turkish Commander, "Allah wasn't willing or they wouldn't have been late." Finally Sam put his foot down and told the Turkish commander, "There are two men now; one is Allah and the other is Sam Williams, and Sam has to be satisfied and Allah wants Sam to be satisfied."[5]

According to Clark, the Turks ever after hit their objectives on time.

While in Korea, Sam became a close adviser, friend, and confidant of South Korean president Syngman Rhee and his wife. He met with President Rhee both at his command post and in Seoul. Their friendship continued until Sam left Korea after the signing of the armistice and was renewed on his return to Korea as Eighth Army deputy commander in 1954. Sam considered his close relationship with Rhee to be the result of Sam's demonstration of loyalty to a South Korean sergeant the first time he met the Rhees—an incident a more tactful man might have avoided at all costs.

The day after Sam arrived at the Twenty-fifth's command

post, he received an invitation to have tea with the Rhees at the presidential palace. Sam discovered that he was the only American present, the other guests being Koreans. He knew the Rhees both spoke English so he introduced himself and exchanged pleasantries. In later years, Sam told the following story:

> I asked the president how he would like to meet one of his sergeants. What a hell of a thing to do! The Rhees looked at each other, and Mrs. Rhee replied, "General Williams, if it will please you, we will be delighted." I went to the parking lot and returned with my South Korean driver-interpreter. We walked up to the president and his wife, and I introduced them to one of their countrymen. I believe it was the first time either of them had ever talked to an ordinary Korean soldier. Now, that soldier, instead of becoming tongue-tied, chatted in a relaxed manner with them. Then Madame Rhee took the sergeant by the arm and filled a plate full of food for him and remained with him until he ate it. When he was finished, we excused ourselves after thanking the president and Mrs. Rhee for inviting us to their reception.
>
> Throughout the time the sergeant was eating and being cared for by Mrs. Rhee, the president just watched in what I believed was amazement.[6]

Sam was once again surprised and pleased to be notified on 19 September 1952 of his promotion to major general. Not only had he regained his star, but now another was pinned on his jacket. Major General Williams wrote of his promotion: "Having had command of the Division for sixty days with no indication of advancement, I had just about come to the conclusion it was one of those things and that no further promotion would come my way. Consequently, to a degree it was a surprise and, needless to say, a welcomed one." (Letter to Col. Allen Kingman, 1 October 1952.) He nearly missed the notification, and little ceremony accompanied the event, as he wrote in October of 1952:

> Almost didn't get notified. Had been sent down to Southern part of Korea to inspect some South Korea training camps, came back to the Corps air strip and had to make an after dark landing with a pilot who didn't know the strip and

without lights, in a narrow valley between mountains. The Corps Commander took me up to his CP and by jeep light pinned on the two stars and, also by jeep light, we walked around the guard of honor and the band. (Letter to Lt. Col. Carl Mann, 15 October 1952.)

By early 1953, General Clark, by then UNC forces commander, was fully involved in trying to find a political solution to the stalemate that existed in Korea. From February through April of 1953, the front had remained generally quiet, but in May, the volume of artillery fire increased. Chinese forces then attacked with regimental-sized units, pressing hard against forward outposts guarding key approaches to Seoul and the south. During May of 1953, the Twenty-fifth Division was defending a wide and active front. General Orders dated 27 June 1953 for the award of the Silver Star to Maj. Gen. Samuel T. Williams state:

In the face of heavy daily mortar and artillery fire falling in an unpredictable pattern on the front lines, and with complete disregard for his personal safety, General WILLIAMS visited every front line position and important combat outpost to personally verify and coordinate the details of each combat post and fighting position. The information gained by his repeated personal visits to the front lines and outposts enabled General WILLIAMS to coordinate the disposition of troops and commanders and soldiers to a heroic labor in fortification which greatly increased the strength and security of the division's positions. General WILLIAMS' gallant conduct and superior professional ability displayed during many contacts with officers and soldiers in front line trenches and on the outposts with utter disregard for his personal safety, was an inspiration to his officers and soldiers and created in them the utmost confidence in their fighting ability.

In early June, General Maxwell Taylor, current Eighth Army commander, directed Sam to the II Republic of Korea (ROK) Corps and told him to assist them in any way necessary. The II Corps was experiencing difficulty because the Chinese had hit them with three divisions, and the corps had been pushed south for two miles by the time Sam arrived. For some unknown reason, the Chinese broke off the attack and did not capitalize on the penetration gains they had made. Sam spent a week with the Koreans, visiting the II Corps' forward positions and becoming acquainted with the South Korean division, regimental, and battalion commanders. He said "knowing them proved very useful later."[7]

"Later" was the first week in July when Sam again received a call from Taylor who told him, "Your friends are once again in trouble. Get over there as soon as you can." Sam gathered as much enemy information as he could, figuring he might be with the II ROK Corps for some time. He was right. When Sam arrived, a deputy liaison officer from Taylor's headquarters gave him orders in which he was named II ROK Corps deputy commander. The II Corps' commander had been disabled with malaria, and, as Taylor wrote in his autobiography, "To give him every assistance, I lent him for use as a deputy corps commander Major General Samuel T. Williams, known throughout the Army under the sinister sobriquet of 'Hangin' Sam' . . . He was an old friend of Leavenworth days for whose professional judgment I had the highest regard. He and [the corps commander] turned out to be a most effective team."[8]

The orders were published with the concurrence of South Korean President Rhee and placed Sam in the South Korean army "chain of command." He was not appointed as an adviser. It is, possibly, the only occasion that an American general officer was placed under a South Korean commander. Sam recalled later that to command six Korean divisions in combat was not difficult even though his Korean commanders did not speak English and he did not have an interpreter. He made sketches in the sand and marks on a map to convey his directions.[9]

On the night of July 13th, three Chinese divisions attacked down the boundary between the II ROK Corps and the U.S. IX Corps. The gains they made were soon consolidated by additional Chinese armies. Sam moved immediately to the front to evaluate the damages. Not satisfied with his ground survey, he took to the air to determine how best to coordinate the defense of his nearly twenty miles of mountainous front. For this act of "extraordinary heroism," Sam received the Distinguished-Service Cross. The General Orders, dated 30 July 1953, describe his helicopter flight:

> Despite the turbulence of the air and the intense ground fire, he directed the pilot to fly low over enemy troop concentrations. Dipping repeatedly to within a few feet of the hostile positions, General WILLIAMS noted the disposition of the foe without regard for the heavy fire directed against his craft. At one point, a bullet ripped through the plastic canopy of the helicopter, narrowly missing him. However, even this did not cause him to turn back. Instead, he passed again and again over the battle area until satisfied that he had gathered sufficient information upon which to base an effective defense.

During his return flight to the II Corps command post, he prepared in his mind a plan of how to stop and then destroy the advancing enemy.

Sam discussed his findings with General Taylor and made tactical recommendations as related to the situation on his front. He then moved to the Sixth ROK Division, which was in trouble on his right front. But twelve days later the fighting ended. The last offensive by either side concluded on 27 July 1953.

General Williams left Korea in early August to return to the United States. But he never got there. On a stop-over in Japan, he called on Clark's headquarters and was surprised to be offered the command of the XVI U.S. Army Corps stationed in northern Japan. He accepted immediately and called for Jewell to join him.

For less than a year, Jewell and Sam experienced the delights of living in Japan. But their pleasant life was interrupted in 1954 when Sam accepted a new job in Korea as commander of the IX Corps. He accepted it because he still thought the communists would violate the truce, and as usual, he wanted to be at the focal point if they again attacked. Jewell remained in Sendai, Japan.

Later that year, while retaining command of the IX Corps,

General Williams was named Eighth Army deputy commander, a position he held until December of 1954. At that time, General Collins, in his final days as the army chief of staff, named General Williams deputy general of the Fourth Army with station at Fort Sam Houston, Texas.

Sam was going home.

(Above left) MAAG briefing during a visit from the Eighth Army, 1959. Gen. Sam Williams is seated in the middle of the front row; Ambassador Elbridge Durbrow, who respected Sam's leadership but felt conflict working with him, sits to Sam's right.

(Above right) General Williams in Vietnam.

(Next page) Field shot of Sam during his tour in Vietnam, 1955–60. Lt. Col. Peter Dul, Sam's aide de camp, is third from the right.

Chapter 11 ☆ ☆ ☆ *Vietnam: 1955–1960*

Sam arrived at Fort Sam Houston in January of 1955 and was given charge of training supervision for the Reserve and National Guard forces located in Texas, New Mexico, Arkansas, Oklahoma, and Louisiana. Gen. I.D. White, Sam's friend from Germany and Korea, was the army commander. Shortly after Sam reported, White was sent to Korea as the Eighth Army commander, and despite being junior to many of the army's major generals serving in the Fourth Army, Sam was named as White's successor.

On 15 September 1955, Major General Williams received his third star. Brig. Gen. James O. Boswell, his friend from the Ninetieth and World War II, wrote to him that month:

> That day in Normandy when you left the division . . .
> you told Dick Stilwell and me that you would never quit and

[would] "come back."

How far can a person come?

Throughout the Army you have a reputation which is unique as a combat soldier, a leader, and as a character.

Please do not ever lose any of them.

In October, General Taylor sent Sam a telegram in which he asked if there were any cogent reason why Sam should not be sent to South Vietnam as chief of its Military Assistance and Advisory Group (MAAG). Taylor told him that his mission would be to organize and train the new republic's army, navy, and air force. Sam replied that he had no objections to a tour in Vietnam, even though he had spent the best part of twelve years abroad. Taylor once had said, probably with tongue in cheek, that a MAAG chief should be a photogenic, linguistically gifted cosmolite with a distinguished record, a polished drawing room technique, a pleasant manner with the press, and a capability for holding his tongue.

He sent Hanging Sam Williams anyway.

Sam later said that the briefings he received from the army before his Vietnam tour were so lengthy and thorough that it was impossible for him to remember half of what he was told. But his memory did retain an incident related to the G2 orientation. The army G2, an old friend of Sam's, took him to his Pentagon G2 offices hidden behind a barrier of several locked and sometimes guarded doors. There, Sam was told that the CIA was going to try to infiltrate his MAAG, and if he discovered such activity, he was to let Army G2 know immediately. "Hells fire," Sam later remarked, "when I finally arrived in Vietnam I was greeted by Col. Ed Lansdale, USAF, who told me he had a team of eleven CIA agents in the country."[1]

An interview given him by the State Department also amused Sam. When he arrived at the State Department offices, he was taken to a public waiting room. Soon, without introduction, a man greeted him and engaged him in conversation. They discussed the weather, President Eisenhower's heart attack, which had occurred a few days earlier, and then he was asked if he could speak French. Sam said "no," and the conversation turned to other matters of little or no importance to Sam. Finally, Sam asked the unidentified man if he knew anything about his interview regarding his move to Vietnam. Sam's unknown chatterer responded, "General, you have just been interviewed." Then he withdrew. "What a hell of a way to operate a U.S. policy-setting department," Sam said.[2]

Before he left Washington, Sam was advised of the parameters of the Geneva Accords, which provided for a free election to be held in Vietnam in July of 1956. He was also told that South Vietnam was going to ignore this provision, believing that the elections in the north would be neither free nor supervised. Consequently, Sam was instructed to be prepared for an attack from the north by raising some type of South Vietnamese armed force and having it ready in less than a year after his arrival.

Sam arrived in Saigon 28 October 1955 where he would remain as chief of MAAG until August of 1960, an unusual length of time for a tour of duty as mentally and physically demanding as it proved to be, as he wrote to H.J. Brees, president of the National Bank of Fort Sam Houston, in late December of 1955: "I'm finding this assignment the most difficult one of any to date. This [is] due to the relationship here between the Vietnamese on one hand and the French on the other. The Americans usually find themselves squeezed by both."

General "Iron Mike" O'Daniel, before passing the reins of responsibility to Sam, briefed Sam on the existing historical conditions that had influenced the MAAG's mission. The Republic of Vietnam was one of the states emerging from the area once known as Indochina. Vietnam and Cambodia, after nearly one hundred years of domination by the French and, more recently, suffering from the aggression of communist Laos, were struggling for survival. They faced a new type of colonialism before they had full independence from the French. The apparent policy of the United States at the time was to assist with the preservation of each independent state in accordance with the democratic belief in the right of all free people to choose their own government. Also, a strong front would check the aggressive Chinese armies to the north, armies still fresh in the minds of those Americans familiar with their activities in South Korea.

In June of 1954, the Geneva Accords were acknowledged by nine of the seven interested nations—Britain, France, Cambodia, Laos, the Soviet Union, China, and Ho Chi Minh's Democratic Republic of Vietnam. The United States and the State of Vietnam "took note" of the agreement. One of the military agreements that placed a heavy burden on O'Daniel was the partitioning of the little country along a demarcation line bordering the seventeenth parallel, resulting in a Communist-controlled north and a noncommunist south. Also, O'Daniel found himself handicapped by the accords because he was unable to have his organization strengthened by the addition of more officers and soldier technicians.

As usual, Sam took time to acquaint himself with key personnel involved in his new assignment. O'Daniel arranged a meeting with Ngo Dinh Diem, who had served as the president of ministers in a government headed by the former Emperor Bao Dai. Dai was ousted by popular vote because Diem, during his fifteen months as president of ministers, had gathered much support for the ideals of a representative government, which he had long advocated. On 26 October 1955, the people joined Diem in proclaiming South Vietnam as the Republic of Vietnam. Diem faced great difficulties in the beginning, however, as he was opposed by various religious sects, politicians of every stripe, and members of his army, including his chief of staff.

Sam immediately liked Diem because of his honesty and his unswerving dedication to the people of Vietnam. Sam felt he was "of high moral character and uncorrupt despite rumors and suggestion of such by his enemies, and too frequently by Americans. I trusted his wisdom and believed him when he told me he was 'just trying to build a country.'"[3]

In briefing Sam, General O'Daniel revealed that Sam's primary work in the beginning was the resettlement of refugees from the north. Conservatively, O'Daniel estimated that 500,000 to a million refugees had come south; thus, tremendous amounts of food, tents, and medical supplies were needed. Supplemented by the Red Cross, religious welfare agencies, and others, O'Daniel used all of his American manpower to accomplish the huge humanitarian demands. Consequently, by the time Sam arrived, little had been done toward organizing a strong military establishment; the existing French organization of the Vietnamese military prevailed.

O'Daniel remained in Vietnam for a short time, which gave Sam the freedom to conduct a country-wide reconnaissance and the opportunity to familiarize himself with the nation's geography. He first went to Hue, an area where he expected battles to develop in July of 1956. He closely examined the boundaries on the west—Laos and Cambodia—as well as the road network. The country had mountains located along the coastal borders and most were heavily forested. It also had swamps, and no part of the delta area was higher than twenty feet above sea level. During his briefings in the Pentagon Sam had been told that Vietnam would be a poor place to fight a war. To that, Sam had replied that he had never seen a good place to fight a war.

Along with the creation of a South Vietnamese army, Sam faced another major problem after O'Daniel left: the need to obtain authorization for sufficient trained personnel to handle the immense quantities of military equipment that the United States had shipped into Vietnam to support the French during France's effort to maintain its Indochina colonies. Various estimates placed the value of the equipment at $700 million to $1.2 billion. Sam's small advisory group of 342 members had little capability to handle or cope with the millions of dollars that were to be returned to the United States. The property was scattered about South Vietnam in unprotected dumps, unguarded and unmaintained. Sam's correspondence soon revealed that the agency blocking increase in personnel was the Department of State, which wanted to continue to abide by the Geneva Accords although they never had been signed by the United States.

Unexpectedly, France and Britain agreed to authorizing additional logistical U.S. personnel after they were told that two members of the International Control Commission—Canada and India—had no objection to the plan's implementation. In the end, the approved plan—Temporary Equipment Recovery Mission

(TERM)—called for 350 additional officers and enlisted personnel. Under Sam, by the end of 1957, only seven of the 350 actually were working on logistical recovery missions; the remainder had been absorbed by MAAG and the Army of the Republic of Vietnam (ARVN). The International Control Commission never voiced disapproval of the clandestine program to strengthen the MAAG–ARVN.

Sam continued to prepare for an attack from the north in which the communists would use conventional forces and tactics. Years later, he modified this approach, but at the time he was aware of the victories over communist forces in Iran, the Philippines, Greece, and Korea. "They can be destroyed in Vietnam too," Sam said.[4]

Sam later would be accused of raising a Vietnamese army in the image of the American army—the wrong approach, according to some. From the beginning, however, Sam convinced Diem that his army did not need a heavy division, an armored division, or an American-style division. Diem and his key senior officers agreed with Sam that they needed a division designed to operate in their country of swamps, plains, paddies, mountains, and jungles. In 1981 Sam said, "It was a simple transition from French-style organizations to ones, at the time, I believed could defeat the communists from the north."[5]

Sam often told the following story in later years: "One French officer said to me, after becoming acquainted with my plans to raise an army and an air force, 'It will be a waste of money to try to form an American-style army. The Vietnamese will not fight.' 'Hell, they just whipped your ass at Dien Bien Phu,' I said to him."[6]

In the beginning of his tour, Sam was certain that the North Vietnamese would conduct a North Korea–type of invasion, but by 1957 he began to change his mind. His turnabout was caused, in part, by the South Vietnamese, who were better equipped and better trained and therefore getting stronger. "I began to think we could handle Comrade Ho's boys," he said years later. Then, simple little insurgency acts began to occur. He continued:

> I began to gather that the hard-core communists were
> coming down, and incidents of murder and casualties in the
> simple farm villages began to happen with a country-wide
> frequency. These communists were coming from the north
> and would contact a member of the Viet Cong who was
> planted in a village a couple of years earlier. From him, they
> would find out the names of the peasants loyal to Diem and
> the army. Come sunrise, the local loyals and their wives and
> their children would be found murdered with their bodies
> violated in the worst possible manner and strewn in the dirt
> road. Terrible. Simple peasants uprising? No, the perpetra-
> tors of such cowardly acts were soldiers of the north, and they
> were assisted in these deeds by their planted communist
> agents.[7]

When Sam arrived in Vietnam, G. Frederick Rheinhardt
was the U.S. ambassador. He and Sam soon established a sound,
working relationship, each recognizing the other's responsibilities and authority. The ambassador was a professional diplomat
who was proud to represent his country. He was quick to share
information and was honest in his approach to understanding
Sam's extraordinary mission of creating a South Vietnamese
army from the military chaos he had inherited.

Sam accepted Rheinhardt as the head of the "Country
Team," which included the chiefs of the various agencies and
missions located in Vietnam—the U.S. Information Service, the
CIA, and the U.S. Operations Mission, as well as an element of the
International Cooperation Administration. Rheinhardt was the
recognized chairman of their meetings, but he exerted little
supervision over any of them. Because of his approach, the
agencies tended to conduct their own programs within the guidance provided by their Washington-based headquarters. Certainly, this was the practice Sam followed, for he responded first
to the Pacific commander in chief in Hawaii and then to his army
chief of staff. Until the arrival of Ambassador Elbridge Durbrow
in March of 1957, Sam worked largely independently of the

Country Team; he limited his response to it by clearing and coordinating only those matters he wanted with little regard to the overall relation of MAAG to the whole.

When Durbrow arrived on the Saigon scene, his rumpled, balding, grinning countenance gave Sam the impression he would be dealing with a Landrum-like character: both were egotistical, shallow in their relationships with subordinates, inclined to exaggerate or cloud the issue, whichever condition favored them at the moment, and both preferred the company of superiors to that of ordinary staff members. Also, Durbrow's language was laced with expressions common to a bilge brig of the French Navy. Sam Williams did not care for vulgar speech unless he was doing the cussing himself.[8]

Whatever the source of Sam's dislike of Durbrow, he demonstrated little respect or consideration for him. Sam said in a post-retirement interview in San Antonio, "I never saw Rhein-hardt do anything that would cause me as an American to be embarrassed, and I never saw him get up, in front of a mixed crowd and strip down to his shorts and put on a belly dance."[9] Although Durbrow's name is not mentioned, the remark suggests the identification of the belly dancer.

Years later, Sam admitted that he was partially responsible for the deterioration in his relationship with the embassy. "Hanging Sam" in some cases lived up to the image of his nickname to the detriment of his mission. His relations with the ambassador in particular touched bottom. His acrimony affected his staff, which felt that no matter their effort, Durbrow or one of his subordinates would override them. Sam continued to believe, and with some justification, that Durbrow was anti-Diem. Furthermore, Sam learned of major projects affecting MAAG that Durbrow did not tell him about.

Sam also thought Durbrow and others of the embassy treated the Vietnamese as inferiors and third-class people. This did not occur in the MAAG; its relationship with Diem until Sam's departure from Vietnam was without friction.

Such excellent relations between MAAG and the representatives of the Vietnamese government are perhaps one of

Sam's best accomplishments during his tour as chief of MAAG–ARVN. Certainly, the relationship between President Diem and General Williams was close and confidential. In a personnel report dated 23 August 1960, Durbrow emphasized Sam's good relationship with Diem at the report's end: "When I was twice asked if Gen. Williams should be extended for another year I concurred primarily because of his seriousness of purpose, the generally fine achievements of MAAG/Viet-Nam under his leadership, and particularly because, in military matters he had gained the confidence of President Diem." Durbrow also described Sam as a "serious," "hard-working," "industrious," officer "who has done an outstanding job here in running a very efficient MAAG." However, the conflict between the two men also showed in the report where Durbrow wrote:

> In regard to tact, judgment on other than military matters and his ability to cooperate with other members of the Country Team, [General Williams] has not been outstanding . . . He seemed to feel that any comment or contrary suggestion was directed at him personally, and often it was necessary to order him to comply with suggestions rather than working out problems on a cooperative basis. I should add that when ordered to take agreed action he complied. Because of his previous experience he apparently found it difficult to show a willingness to see the other angles in the problem, which often were over-riding. This, in my opinion, impaired his judgment of the over-all picture.

Through Sam's leadership, the foundation was laid for the Vietnamese armed forces. His efforts and creative talents resulted in the establishment of a joint army, navy, and air force General Staff; the establishment of an army Central Command and four corps commands; the development of uniformed tables of organization; the creation of a military school system, which included a military academy and a Command and General Staff School; and the organization of an ARVN logistical system.

Senators Albert Gore and Gail W. McGee held extensive "executive hearings" in Saigon, 7–8 December 1959. In a report of their findings, they were sharply critical of the United States

Operation Mission (USOM) in Vietnam. Both pointed at USOM for poor management, faulty administration, and indifferent custodianship of the U.S. economic aid to Vietnam. U.S. Ambassador Durbrow was taken to task for failing to keep adequately abreast of information on various phases of the program, for lack of proper supervisory effort, and for an apparent inability to exert required leadership over concerted, coordinated Country Team efforts. The U.S. Military Assistance Advisory Group, Vietnam, and Vietnamese President Diem were credited with key roles in the development of effective, hard-hitting, balanced armed forces within the young country. Of the American agencies in Vietnam, MAAG fared the best during Gore and McGee's hearings.

At the beginning of the hearings' second session, Gen. Sam Williams, participating in the hearings for the first time, engaged in a spirited exchange with Gore after the senator's repeated interruption of his testimony. From then on, Sam was treated deftly and with circumspection by the two investigating senators.

By 1960, sixty-two-year-old Sam Williams was a tired officer. His five-year tour in Vietnam weighed heavily on him, and he was ready to return home. He had been extended well beyond his required retirement date because of requests by President Diem to Eisenhower, who approved Sam's extension of service on two occasions.

General Samuel T. Williams' active service to his nation as a member of its military forces ended when his retirement orders were read during a simple ceremony at MAAG Headquarters in Saigon, 31 August 1960. The ceremony included awarding him his second Distinguished-Service Medal for his meritorious achievements in Vietnam, as well as for recognition of his nearly forty-four years of unfaltering service and dedication.[10] The orders conclude by emphasizing Sam's dedication to training his men to be the best they could be:

> During his entire service, his main interest has been in
> developing forces under his command into a high state of
> combat efficiency controlled by a hard corps of highly trained
> professional officers and noncommissioned officers. . . . In his

numerous command assignments, he at all times displayed intense interest in the development of the individual noncommissioned officer. He consistently required high performance standards of officers and noncommissioned officers and inspired them to do their best work through his example.

Official U.S. Army photograph of Lt. Gen. Samuel T. Williams taken in 1957.

Chapter 12 ☆ ☆ ☆ *Taps*

Lt. Gen. Samuel Tankersley Williams, U.S. Army, retired, listened to the bugled notes of "Taps" as they drifted across Fort Sam Houston's parade ground.

It was 25 April 1984.

Sam turned off the reading lamp above his army hospital bed. As the softness of sleep came, he recalled that within the first few days of wearing an army uniform in 1916, he was stopped by an officer when he left a road to cut across the parade ground. The lieutenant said, "Soldier, keep off the grass. We do not walk on this field because it is our parade ground."

Other memories arose—Major Owsley of Denton, Captain Harris of the Texas Militia, and Captain McNair of the First Camper days. The long journey to France and the episode with Major Collins of the 359th. Landrum was his carbon copy. Benning and Leavenworth came into focus. Wonder where Von Schell is now, and Smith? Woolfley was in Louisiana. Loyal faces paraded by, great sergeants, Butler, Hill, Mercer, and Dobol.

Great general officers, too. Max, and Creighton and Huebner, Milburn and Van Fleet, General Marshall, and Dick Stilwell, who made four stars.

Good night, Jewell.

Come on, Hoss. Let's take a walk.

The day is done. Night has come.

WILLIAMS

Lt. Gen. Samuel T. Williams, U.S. Army Ret., died Thursday, 26 April 1984. He was 86. Born 25 August 1897 in Denton, Texas, he earned the nickname "Hanging Sam" for his somber command and disciplinary standards.

Williams began his nearly forty-five years of service in May 1916 with the Texas Militia. Wounded twice in battle, General Williams was awarded every army decoration for valor, except the Medal of Honor. He landed with the Ninetieth Division at Utah beach during the invasion of Europe in 1944. He commanded the Twenty-fifth Division in Korea and finished his service in August 1960 as chief of the Military Assistance and Advisory Group to Vietnam, where he was a trusted adviser to South Vietnam's President Ngo Dinh Diem.

General Williams leaves Jewell, his wife of nearly sixty-three years, as his survivor, along with his sister, Ida Henderson.

Internment will be held with full military honors at the Fort Sam Houston Cemetery, Monday, April 30th.

(Next page) In 1955, on his way to Vietnam, General Williams gathered at Schofield Barracks, Hawaii, with ex–Blue Spaders and former Tough Ombres.

Chapter 13 ✩ ✩ ✩ *A Khaki Legend:*
Sam Remembered

After more than a year of gathering material for this biography, my filing cabinets were filled, and today, the volumes of voluntary letters from those whose lives were touched by Sam T. Williams continue to arrive. This mail has revealed that Sam was a multifaceted character: an internationally and well-known military professional who generated deep feelings of respect, or admiration, maybe distaste, or enthusiasm, and sometimes fear within those his presence touched. Amazingly, I did not receive a single piece of vituperation or degrading comment about Sam. Frankly, I expected a woeful note or two from the widows or wives of men who had faced the indignation of "Hanging Sam."

Many of the observations made by my correspondents and their stories, comments, or anecdotes remain another shade of the character of a soldier we call Sam.

The following letter, written by retired Lt. Gen. Ruben Jenkins, was mailed to an officer scheduled for service with General Williams in South Vietnam. He had asked Jenkins about Sam's nature, and in July of 1956, General Jenkins gave this reply:

It was good to get your recent note and to know that you are to join my good and close friend, Sam Williams. I have known him intimately for many years, and I hold few men in so high a personal admiration and respect, as a man and as a commander, as I do him. He is the best trainer of troops (including officers) that I have EVER known (and that is something hard for an old dog like me to say about anybody); and as a fighting man, well I may have seen his equal a time or two (but for the moment they slip my memory) but I have NEVER seen any better, anywhere—under any circumstances; and I have seen him in some tight spots, believe me, as a division commander and as a Korean Corps commander.

You will (if you do not already know it) find him coldly ruthless in his demands; as coldly impersonal and "dead pan" as a dead salmon, insofar as his business is concerned. He is better known (by nickname) as "Hanging Sam," as you have probably learned, but I never knew him to "hang" anybody; but I have known several who were sure at the time that he was certainly going to "hang" them, yet never did. But he has no hesitancy, none at all, in relieving a subordinate for manifest inefficiency; and the subordinate who thinks otherwise may someday suddenly find that he has made the mistake of his life!!! Yet, NEVER has he been accused by a subordinate or by a superior, or even suspected, of having dealt unjustly with any man regardless of his station or position in his command. To me, his one objective in life always seemed to be "make every man an officer, and every unit better than they are"—and he does a job of it. And along with this tough side of him you will find one of the finest senses of humor and brightest and most humorous dispositions you will ever see. Soldiers worship him for what he is; while officers admire and respect him for what he is, but fear him for what he is NOT. I always found it a rather humorous situation.

Sam commanded the Twenty-sixth Infantry Regiment for nearly five years. During the years from February 1946 through the middle months of 1950, he became the dominant figure in the command and training environment of the U.S. Army in Europe. He used his authority with confidence because he was sure that the goals he set were achievable and essential for the regiment's development. Capt. Don Rivette, who served with the Blue Spaders in World War II and later when they were stationed in Bamberg, noted, "I think 'Hanging Sam' was a lot like Patton. Sam, like Patton, knew if you demanded the impossible that the impossible became a certainty. Additionally, Sam knew that every soldier had a reserve that could be called for that extra effort." (Letter to the author, April 1985.)

While Sam commanded the Blue Spaders, he was always aware of his responsibility to develop junior officers and enlisted leaders. This responsibility was pleasurable for Sam because it challenged him to recognize young platoon leaders for future professional development—a maturing process that would be completed years later. Of course, his interest in a particular junior officer was a secretive one, for he could never show any sign of favoritism or indulgence. The number one Blue Spader used varied methods to watch the progress of junior officers in the regiment. He reviewed every officer efficiency report before its dispatch; he observed young officers conduct field training; he directed the assignment of one or another to a particular job, both to get it done and to have the opportunity to watch the lieutenant work under pressure; he reassigned those he felt were not challenged in an ordinary position; he discussed officers assigned to a battalion with the battalion's commander; and he quietly evaluated the information given him by trusted noncommissioned officers.

The following letter from retired Maj. Gen. Fred E. Karhohs explores the experience of being a beginning infantry officer, as well as Sam's interest in officer development (letter to the author, January 1985):

I had the pleasure of serving about two years with the 26th Infantry at Bamberg during the years 1948–1950. In my opinion, the "Blue Spader" Regiment was the finest Infantry Regiment of its day. I personally learned more about what an officer should and shouldn't do than at any time in my 30-year military career. In those days in Bamberg we literally lived and breathed the Regiment and its leader, Colonel Williams.

For example, we had excellent regimental-level athletic competitions throughout Germany in that period. The entire Regiment supported its basketball, football and boxing teams along with the more traditional military events of rifle, pistol and other gunnery matches. It was simply great fun to work every day!

Every Saturday morning we would have a regimental parade—to include the 26th Infantry's Scout Dog Platoon (one or more of whom would occasionally "break ranks" and tangle with Colonel Williams' dog Hoss). In those days, the Drum and Bugle Corps paraded daily through the battalion areas with their stirring music at reveille and retreat formations . . . .

My first assignment upon reaching the 26th Infantry was as the Platoon Leader of "F" Company's Weapons Platoon, a job I thoroughly enjoyed. Sometime in the summer of 1949, I was called into the Regimental Adjutant, Captain Ross I. Donnelly's office. Captain Donnelly informed me that I would be "trying out" for the Regimental football team. I informed Captain Donnelly that I wasn't interested in playing football and that I had a Platoon to take care of. He informed me that the choice wasn't mine since Colonel Williams had read my "Form 66" and noted that I had played football in college. Within two weeks I was in practice sessions with the 26th Infantry's football team, and I became its quarterback.

Prior to the 1949 football season the 2nd Battalion went to Grafenwöhr to participate in Regimental field exercises. In addition to my football "duties," I was appointed officer in charge of all the "rear echelon" personnel of the 2nd Battalion who for one reason or another did not accompany the Battalion to its late summer training session.

My daily supervision of these soldiers consisted essentially of visiting the Battalion command post in the morning before the morning football practice session and again later in the day after the afternoon football practice session. I would check in and ask the duty Sergeant "How are things going?", sign a few papers and depart to my quarters in the National Hotel.

One day, approximately two weeks after the 2nd Battalion had departed Bamberg, I received a message from a runner to report to Colonel Williams immediately. I changed into fresh uniform and proceeded to Regimental Headquarters. Captain Donnelly looked a bit grim and said, "Look out— the 'old man' is mad." I knocked on the door, entered when directed, stopped about three paces before his desk, stood at attention, saluted and reported. His first words were "You are less a leader than a goddamn stable hand!

"I thought that you were one of my best lieutenants but you have been doing an absolutely crappy job of supervising those soldiers in the 2nd Battalion. This morning two of your young men threw a brick through a window in downtown Bamberg. They were drunk, disgraced themselves and the Regiment. Now, get your ass out of here and get things squared away!"

My answer, of course, was "Yes Sir!" I opened his office door, closed it softly and walked out across the hall to Captain Donnelly's office. I said, "Captain Donnelly, I am quitting the football team." He responded, "You can't quit. You're the quarterback." I said, "It's either that or my Army career. I have no choice. I quit!"

I returned to my quarters, got my field clothing along with field bedding and headed directly to the 2nd Battalion headquarters. I set up a bunk in an office and called a meeting of all unit sergeants. I told them that this afternoon I would publish a training schedule that would be effective immediately. Among other things, I personally held daily reveille and retreat formations. I visited every soldier at his job every day. Furthermore, I issued damn few passes and any requested for Bamberg required my personal approval. I stayed at my post day and night and intended to do so until the battalion returned from Grafenwöhr. I was determined not to be stood at attention again by "Hanging Sam."

Four days later, during my fourth consecutive evening Retreat formation . . . the ranking Sergeant . . . looked over my shoulder and said quietly, "Sir, Colonel Williams is heading this way."

With the troops at attention, I did a smart about face and reported to him. With a wry and barely perceptible smile,

Hanging Sam said to me, "The soldiers look great—you've learned your lesson—now get your ass back on the football field."

I responded, "Yes Sir!"

Throughout the rest of my military career during which I commanded Companies, Battalions, Brigades and served as an Assistant Division Commander, I never forgot the lesson that Colonel Williams taught me: If you are assigned a mission, no matter how insignificant it might seem, you simply must do everything possible to carry it out in the full spirit and intent desired by the Commander. And more importantly, you must *personally* do everything you can to insure that the mission is accomplished. That simple lesson taught me in Bamberg by Colonel Williams in 1949, was the best thing that ever happened to me. For that experience and the many other examples of outstanding leadership traits demonstrated by Colonel Williams [I'm] proud to have served in his command. He was truly a soldier's soldier!

The following tells the story of Col. Frank Plummer's introduction to the Twenty-sixth Infantry (letter to the author, September 1987):

In March of 1949 I arrived at the Excelsior Hotel in Bamberg, Germany, a confident, enthusiastic second lieutenant. In my briefcase I had orders directing me to join the 26th Infantry Regiment for a one-year tour designed to evaluate my performance as a potential Regular Army Officer. The evaluation process meant serving in a variety of closely supervised leadership positions, and under different rating and grading officers. Following a year of such duty, individual records, tests and performance were measured against the records of other Army-wide participating officers. The reward for your hard work was selection for a regular commission. The process known as "Competitive Tour" was a fair, difficult, rigorous test of ability and potential. While I am delighted to say I was accepted for the RA commission, my initial entry into the 26th Infantry Regiment, with it's commander "Hanging Sam," caused me to have doubts as to my immediate sanity, and my long-range military ambitions.

My doubts began to flourish my first evening in the Excelsior, a hotel operated for bachelor and visiting officers.

Immediately, young officers serving in the Blue Spade Regiment told me the current horror stories, all of which centered on a diabolical colonel named Williams. It appeared he ate second johns for breakfast, captains for lunch, and field grade officers for dinner. He held no brook for [any] officer—junior or senior—who failed to meet his standards. No mention [was made] of what the standards were, yet I did gather the qualifications for an infantry officer were unchanging; only perfection was accepted by the Colonel, and then, rarely. I listened, but such exaggeration was commonplace on the entry of a young, unproven officer.

Nonetheless, when I went to the Regimental Headquarters the next morning I was appropriately adorned with the proper patches and crests—all borrowed. After reporting to the Adjutant, Captain Ross I. Donnelly, I was told by him to take a seat. From it I could see the door of the office belonging to Colonel Samuel T. Williams. Almost immediately I heard loud shouting taking place within his office. Suddenly the Colonel's office door opened and a Captain of Cavalry was backing out as a finger of a red-faced Colonel snapped in his face. The finger belonged to Colonel Williams, who shouted, "Get off this post in ten minutes."

The Captain barely cleared the office threshold as Colonel Williams slammed its door in his face.

The Cavalry Captain, attempting to regain his composure, turned to the Adjutant and said, "I will not be treated like this. All I said to him was that I would have preferred assignment to a [cavalry] unit. At that, he began to yell and raise hell. What the hell is the matter with him—is he crazy? I have official orders from the Department of the Army. He cannot do this to me. I am an officer."

"You have eight minutes remaining," remarked Captain Donnelly without a change of demeanor.

The booted Captain continued to mutter and make motions toward the door of the commander.

"You are down to seven minutes," said Captain Donnelly as a burly Assistant Adjutant and a muscular Sergeant appeared on the scene as if called.

"Six," said the Adjutant.

"Your bags and foot locker are off-post and you are departing now!" said the Assistant. The Captain of Cavalry, stifling another verbal assault, marched stiffly in front of his escorts down the hall and out of the building.

Within a minute the Officer of the Day called Captain Donnelly [and told him] that the Cavalry Captain was no longer on the Infantry Post. Donnelly, as if it was routine to do such, notified the Colonel that the Cavalry Officer was gone. My knees were trembling and I knew what was causing them to shake and my hands to sweat. It was obvious—I was next on "Hanging Sam's" scaffold.

Colonel Plummer was an outstanding officer whom Sam never found in disfavor. Nor did Plummer have to face the uncertainties of a personal interview with Sam. But Sam's volatile nature could explode unexpectedly and with punishing results. Once in 1949, the Blue Spaders were preparing for their annual range firing season, and Sam ordered all officers to undergo a refresher course in the basics of rifle marksmanship. During the instructional period, Sam discovered a lieutenant who had put on his rifle sling incorrectly. He assembled the officers, and held the poor company officer up to ridicule. "Hanging Sam" would not accept the fact that a lieutenant of infantry would err in putting on a rifle sling. He subjected the young officer to some powerful and celebrated criticism and then dismissed him with the statement, "Don't let the sun set on you tonight in my regiment or in Bamberg." Understanding comrades helped the respected officer with his unexpected travel and change of station orders.

Col. Norman H. Bykerk added these observations about Sam's treatment of new officers (letter to the author, September 1985):

STW usually knew considerably about an incoming officer. He studied their records prior to interviewing them. It was not unusual for him to question a Military Academy graduate with "What was the number of your Officer Candidate School Class?" Conversely, he would inquire of a newly assigned graduate "What was your class standing at West Point?" Such questions made the incoming officer think and talk on his feet. This gave Sam a pressure profile of the young man. . . .

He never vented his full indignation on anyone but those

he considered having outstanding leadership ability and great command potential.

But "Hanging Sam" was always fundamentally concerned for and cared about his soldiers and officers, which made an impression on Command Sgt. Maj. Ted Dobol:

> When Colonel Williams left a regimental NCO call, he never was in a hurry. He would stop, talk to an NCO, ask about his family or how many of his platoon soldiers were skilled marksmen or experts in their specialty.
> He made NCOs aware of their responsibilities. . . .Yet I never observed him talking to a noncommissioned officer with anything less than patience and understanding. He seemed to give a soldier a quiet sense of confidence in himself. The soldier always felt good after talking to Colonel Williams.
> He seemed to exhilarate them somehow. I could never understand this quality for it was an exceptional one. Just by his presence he motivated soldiers to do better. When he talked to a soldier he concentrated on what the soldier said. He was completely absorbed with that NCO at that time. He listened to the soldier. While I know many officers lost their voices when confronted by the "Old Man," he never made a soldier feel less than comfortable on a one-to-one basis. If an NCO just said "Yes sir" or "No sir," Colonel Williams made them talk. He asked where they joined the army, how many brothers they had, what their Dad's work was. He made soldiers talk to him, but he never embarrassed them. Blue Spade soldiers loved him. He was a truly wonderful officer leader. He was a soldier. We were proud of him and felt honored to serve as an NCO under him. (From interviews with and letters to the author, 1966, 1973, 1984, and 1985.)

At some point in his career, Sam acquired a reputation for being mildly stingy. Before returning to Washington from Europe in 1944, he bought a field coat and boots from the Quartermaster Clothing Sales Store because he knew they were less expensive than in the United States. Perhaps a penchant for penny-pinching developed during the many years he served as a supply officer and as a company commander responsible for costly government property. He knew the necessity of making every bullet count, both on the battlefield and on the training ranges. As his career developed, he accepted the reality of strict property control and the management of federal resources.

In the closing weeks of assignment in South Vietnam, General Williams ordered a 1961 two-door Cadillac delivered upon his arrival in San Antonio. He specified that the new car should not be equipped with a heater, "for San Antonio is warm enough so that a car heater is unnecessary. Why pay for something that won't be used?"

He was convinced by staff members that the heater was essential for defrosting and ventilation. Only after considerable correspondence did he agree to pay for one.

—*Mr. Woodson H. Harris* (letters to the author, February 1980, July 1985, and August 1987)

But Sam also could be a generous and giving man:

General Williams was frugal in his money practices. How surprised I was to learn that he designated 5 soldiers— 3 enlisted men and 2 officers—to receive $10,000 each from his estate. A remarkable man, a loyal and generous man.

—*Mr. Patrick H. Reagan,* Executor, S.T. Williams Estate (letters to the author, 1985–1987)

Uncle Sam never forgot the church of his Sunday School days—the First Presbyterian. From the first year of his enlistment he gave it an offering. His checks became larger as he was promoted. In the final years when he lived in San Antonio, they became substantial. Our church records reflect his thoughtfulness and continuing support.

—*Mr. Woodson H. Harris*

Other, more personal, memories included:

In 1930 Sam and Jewell visited my father and stepmother in South America. The elevation of our town was about 6,500 feet. My folks planned a duck hunting trip to a lake 2,000 feet above where we lived. The lake could be reached only by foot or on muleback. My dad gave Uncle Sam his finest mule. Sam became indignant, refused to ride the mule and requested a horse for the trip. The horse was skittish. It kept trying to

turn back on the narrow trail. The treacherous winding trail was only mule-wide and the drop below was nearly perpendicular. I did not know until years later that Uncle Sam was frightened. "Worse than war" was the way he put it.
—*Mrs. George J. Merriman* (letter to the author, June 1985)

My wife and I were guests in Sam and Jewel's home many times. They were wonderful to us—a perfect host and hostess. There was but one rule that guests were required to honor twice a day. Sam listened to the evening news at 6:00 p.m. and again at 10. Guests, and especially those who were also viewing the news, were required to remain absolutely quiet during the broadcast and that "no talking" was extended through the commercials also. Should a guest unthinkingly speak during the program he became the focal point of one of General Williams' steely-eyed stares.
—*Mr. Charles Spear* (letter to the author, March 1988)

Sam Williams loved his country, soldiers, the army, his family and animals, although not necessarily in that order. During his childhood in Denton, he became knowledgeable about farm work and animals—especially horses. When he was thirteen, he "hired out" as a farmhand during the summer months at fifty cents a day plus board and became experienced at handling horses. In 1952, Sam wrote to Gen. Tom Hennen: "Frankly, I haven't been on a horse since 1942 and, strange to say, the idea of riding doesn't appeal to me. I don't understand this myself as my primary recreation from 1922 to 1942 was built entirely around horse riding of some description, as you well know."

During the period of time Sam mentioned, his annual efficiency reports contained many favorable remarks about his polo-playing ability and skills as a horseman. In later years, he became fond of dogs, especially his German Shepherd "Hoss," as being better suited to his daily schedule.

My earliest memory of Uncle Sam was seeing him roping calves on a farm near Denton. My cousins were amazed at his skill and agility. I could not understand how a soldier could do those things, for he was not a cowboy.
—*Mrs. George J. Merriman*

At Fort Benning when he was an advanced course student [1930–31], he played the number four position on the Infantry School Polo team. He was violent in his riding and masterful in his horsemanship. Following a game he would critique every move made by his opponents. He was aggressive yes, but he never endangered his mounts nor did he have much regard for his opponents or their horses.

—*Brig. Gen. James Boswell* (author's interviews, 5–6 October 1986, 3–4 October 1987)

My battalion was ordered to Grafenwöhr for winter training in bitter cold weather. My wife, in Bamberg, met Mrs. Williams walking Sam's dog.

My wife remarked. "Colonel Williams didn't take Hoss with him?"

"Oh no my dear,"replied Jewell. "Sam told me that it was much too cold in Grafenwöhr for a dog."

—*Lt. Jack Moyer* (letter to the author, June 1986)

His dog Hoss was an excellent barometer of how things were when you were called to his office. If Hoss was lying at his feet or near his chair the coast was clear. If Hoss was in a distant corner—beware!

—*Col. Norman H. Bykerk* (author's interview, December 1985)

In 1957 my husband was appointed head of the Military Assistance Group in Cambodia. One stop on our journey to that country was Saigon. When we debarked, there to our surprise was General Williams and his wife, Jewell. We were treated royally by them and we were delighted to be guests in their home. . . .

General Williams' old German Shepherd, "Hoss" I believe, was around, a gimpy old dog whose hips were diseased. Later on during our tour, we visited General Williams at his request, but Jewell was in the States. By this time the old German Sheherd had died, and had been replaced by a French poodle. General Williams claimed the poodle was a sissy kind of a dog, but [indicated] he was somewhat attached to it.

. . . One evening when we were watching a movie in the living room. . . . All of a sudden that poodle came racing into the room from the garden and following right on his heels was a large rabbit!

General Williams said, "Did you see that? Nobody ever believes me when I tell them that. . . . Now I have two witnesses, who can testify to the truth of it."

—*Mrs. Dottie Hartshorn* (letter to the author, April 1988)

Many people who had worked with or under Sam Williams during his long military career wrote and reminisced about his character and the time they had spent with him.

Sam Williams and I were fellow students at the Command and Staff School (now College) during the two-year course. I acquired an early liking for Sam approaching admiration. When he spoke he made sense. His grades were not of the highest, but he had no reason to fear for them.

—*Gen. Maxwell D. Taylor* (letter to the author, July 1985)

At times I think, Sam Williams tended to command platoons and companies to the detriment of the usual chain of command, but I also think that this was caused by his overwhelming desire to reestablish himself after his WWII experience. I could not run a regiment as Sam did, but who can fault success.

—*Col. Erwin "Biff" Nilsson* (letter to the author, August 1985)

When I reported to Colonel Williams he was the commander of the 378th Infantry Regiment stationed at Camp Swift, Texas. I had just recently graduated from the Military Academy and having been taught by many senior officers at the Point I felt no trepidation as I stood in front of his desk, having given him my best salute. Williams acknowledged my salute, glared at me with a piercing look, and said with just a hint of a sneer, "West Point, huh?"

He continued, "There are now two Regular Army officers in this regiment: you, the lowest ranking second lieutenant, and me, its only colonel and its commanding officer. Do not expect any goddam favors from me, Lieutenant Ulsaker!"

. . . About the end of January, 1943, Colonel Williams received word that he was to be promoted to brigadier general and transferred to the 90th Division. The day he departed he held an officers call. He shook hands with each officer of the

378th Infantry regiment, thanking each for his support and wished all the best of fortune in combat. I know a number of my fellow officers were glad to see old Sam depart. My thinking was otherwise for I knew that I had learned more in the four months I was under his supervision than I would have under a less rough, caustic and demanding colonel. He had not yet become known as "Hanging Sam," but when I heard he was being called that in later years I clearly understood why.

—*Col. Carl C. Ulsaker* (letter to the author, August 1986)

General Williams was being briefed on the defense of Hokaido, when the G-3 stated that a certain regiment would land on Beach Red at 0600 hours.

"How are they going to get there?" asked the General.

"The Navy will transport them," replied the briefer.

"Has this plan been coordinated with the Navy?" asked the General.

"No sir," admitted the briefer.

"You are fired," concluded "Hanging Sam."

The officer, a Regular Army colonel, was out of the CP within 24 hours. I didn't hear this exchange. I do know the briefing officer left HQ abruptly. The currency of such stories explain the durability of the epithet, "Hanging Sam."

—*Maj. Gen. Charles C. Case* (letter to the author, June 1985)

On two occasions as a captain I attended briefings in his office. Once a lieutenant who was doing the briefing said, "I feel that . . ." Hanging Sam stood up, walked to the briefer, grabbed the briefer's arm with some obvious force, and said to the briefer, "Son, you feel my hand on your arm, don't you? You meant to say, 'I believe,' didn't you?" The young briefing officer agreed with General Williams and so did I.

In fact to this day I'm careful not to confuse feeling with believing.

—*Lt. Gen. Edward A. Partain* (letter to the author, August 1985)

My comments pertaining to General Williams are based on an association of some 37 years and includes peacetime service in the Army, plus combat and retirement. As the saying goes, they broke the mold when he came along.

In my judgment his greatest attributes were hard work, honesty and attention to detail. While some may say the hard work in some instances was unnecessary, no one can say he worked harder than the general.

He could not and would not tolerate complacency at any level. Honesty was a code he lived by, and in this regard there was no compromise. Some could and did criticize him for paying too much attention to detail, yet the most severe critic was aware that he was the most knowledgeable individual in his unit, no matter its size.

His capacity to absorb and retain information was prodigious. In his final years he was slowed by a heart condition, but mentally it was full speed ahead.

Perhaps the most astounding thing about General Williams is the willingness of those who served with him to testify that they became better soldiers or officers for having served with him.

—Lt. Col. Peter Dul (letters to the author, January, April 1985; August 1987; September 1989)

Recently I heard that Sam had a heart pacemaker implanted in his chest. That surprised me for I never believed he had a heart.

—Former Blue Spader (letter to the author, 1984)

Sometime in his young adulthood, Sam Tankersley Williams traveled from his home in Denton, Texas, to the state fair in Dallas. It so happened, the first person that caught his eye was a soldier.

The soldier, dressed in the uniform of the day, wore a campaign hat with leather chin strap, leggings, and had a Colt forty-five hanging on his hip. Sam Williams said, "Hot Damn, that's what I want to be!" He never changed his mind the rest of his life. In 1916 he joined the Texas Militia, and in a short time was on the Mexican border facing Pancho Villa.

Thus began the illustrious military career of a great and gallant soldier. He rose through the ranks from Private to Brigadier General, was unjustly "busted" to Colonel, and came back to earn three stars—a feat that seldom, if ever, has been duplicated.

Sam Williams was a true task master, and could be tough, but he was fair. It was my pleasure to be his first aide de camp—in training in the states, in the invasion of Normandy,

and in the battle for the Contentin Peninsula. Not being an
arm chair or dugout general, day after day in battle, we were
with the leading elements of the leading company attack. He
would "dress down" a regimental commander or private in top
fashion if either was not doing his job. Always with the Will to
Win, he did not say "You go," but, "Let's Go!"

Sam Williams had a bark and bite, but there never was a
more courageous, gallant, and dedicated soldier. He was a
wonderful human being and a true American patriot.

—*Carl B. Everett* (letter to the author, August 1989)

Sam Williams had a profound influence on my life—not
only while serving with him, but forever after and to this day.

When I first came under the influence of Sam Williams it
was at Camp Barkley, Texas, outside of Abilene. The year was
1943. I was 18 and he was 46. At that time he was a Brigadier
General and the ADC (Assistant Division Commander) of the
90th Division and I a very green and eager Second Lieutenant
and Platoon leader in the 359th Infantry. . . . He was often
critical of our work yet never in a destructive way. He shared,
by way of making a point, his own World War I battle experiences. He never talked down to us. We sure as hell listened
when he did have something to say.

I don't recall if he was referred to as Hanging Sam in
those early days. I believe his nickname came later during the
Constabulary days in Germany after World War II. I'm not
sure. I do remember that he was intolerant of incompetence,
but also very warm and helpful to those subordinates whom
he admired and liked. . . .

Sam behaved brilliantly in combat. He did not fortify
himself with whiskey as some did. During an attack by the
badly decimated 3rd Battalion 357th Infantry against
Gourbesville in Normandy I saw him use his folding stock
carbine to out-duel a German gun that was kicking up sparks
all over the road at his feet. The fact that he couldn't see
worth a damn was finally revealed to both Everett and me on
this day. It placed a hell of an extra burden on us for we
thought that he was all-seeing. Needless to say he made
better soldiers of us all by this example on this and other
occasions.

I was also present when he was relieved, sent to the rear,
and busted from Brigadier General to Colonel, all because
some higher incompetent was trying to save his own skin. A

lesser man would have cashed in his chips then. Not so Sam.

I do not recall that he ever dwelled on this misfortune. Instead, he swallowed hard this great disappointment and got to work. He never looked back, and proved his worth over again by regaining his lost star and adding two more, to boot.

I am aware that he was ruthless and caused some careers to collapse, particularly among some senior officers. I am aware also that on occasions he bullied people he perceived to be incompetent. He felt no compunction to relieve those whom he believed to be deserving of such a fate.

. . .the last time I was to see the old man I was in Schofield Barracks, Hawaii. He wished to see all of us who served him in the past and to have a picture made. The group was made up mostly of ex-Blue Spaders (26th Infantry Regiment) and Tough Ombres (90th Division). We as a group (there were 14 of us) were a proud group. We were certain that we were better men for having been touched by this remarkable self-made man.

I have that picture in my home and it reminds me almost daily of him and my other comrades in arms. All of us I am sure have stood a little taller for having served "Hanging Sam."

—*Lt. Col. Eames L. Yates* (interviews with and letters to the author, 1986–87)

Finally, an anecdotal look at Sam would not be complete without some of his own words:

If loyalty was piss you could not collect a chamber pot full in the State Department. State fellows are loyal to their political party, their Ivy League school, but mostly they are loyal to themselves. They are not called on to demonstrate fidelity to the nation and if they were caused to do so many would decline. They serve without accountability for their actions nor are they threatened with dismissal or relief if they fail. They hide behind the pretext of "policy" and shovel semantical shit without having responsibility for the life of a single American.

It has amused me that when a world situation calls for mature, objective evaluation, the White House will call for a military senior to handle the matter. (Interview with the author, 1976.)

I enjoyed my service with the 26th Infantry Regiment and believe it to have been, at the time we were serving in Bamberg, probably the best-trained infantry regiment in the Army. General Milburn had been a battalion commander in the 29th Infantry Regiment at Fort Benning when I was a captain in that regiment. The 29th at the time had an outstanding reputation as it was the only war strength regiment in the Army and was the demonstration regiment for the Infantry School. One day at Bamberg I remarked to General Milburn that it was my purpose to bring the 26th up to the standards of the old 29th. His pleasing remark was the "Blue Spaders are better right now than the 29th ever was," or words to that effect. (Letter to Col. Charles R. Wright, June 1982.)

I think it would be good for the Army if our officers were more demanding of themselves first, their subordinates second, and then, their troops. It is difficult for me to recall the name of any officer who was free and easy, and indifferent, who ever won a major battle or campaign. (Speech, U.S. Military Academy, 8 May 1961.)

A good esprit de corp is especially important for the Army and particularly for the Infantry. The ship's captain can turn his ship around and steam toward combat and all of his sailors must go with him whether they want to or not. The captain of a bomber heads into his bomb run and his crew must stay with the aircraft—they have no choice.
But when the infantry platoon leader gives his signal "Follow Me," it is up to every soldier whether he moves ahead or merely leans forward in his foxhole. Soldiers are subject to special stresses when they know there is nothing between them and the enemy but the muzzles of their rifles and their leaders. That is the moment of truth of leadership and that is the true test of its off-spring, esprit de corps. (Speech, U.S. Military Academy, 8 May 1961.)

It has been my good fortune to have served with several different divisions and observe several others in which esprit de corps was as high or higher than any comparable unit in the Navy, the Air Force or the Marines. As an example more than 390 noncommissioned officers and soldiers of the 1st Infantry Division in Germany volunteered and came to Korea to fight in the 25th Infantry Division in 1952–1953. I doubt if that impressive deed has ever been duplicated by our Sister Services. If it had been we would have heard about it. (Speech, U.S. Military Academy, 8 May 1961.)

This last extract is from a letter by Sam to a major serving in the Ninetieth Infantry Division who was being boarded for inefficiency. The major asked Sam to verify that he had complied with an order that was prompted by Sam's remark to the division chief of staff. Sam declined to do so because he was unaware of the action. Sam, himself the victim of a gross injustice, wrote to him on 27 October 1944:

From your address I naturally assume that you are no longer with the division and are up for reassignment. This is probably very unpleasant for you but if advice is in order, I suggest that you accept it as one of those things that can happen, justly or not, and go ahead with your new assignment, whatever it may be and do the best you can.

The Army is awfully big, and there are bound to be injustices where so many are concerned. We must accept this and keep pitching to the best of our ability.

Chapter Notes

Chapter 1

1. Williams, letter to Ida Williams Henderson, 18 January 1963. After his retirement, Sam's sisters encouraged him to write down his reminiscences, which he did in letters written to them. Mrs. Henderson kindly made these letters available to the author.

2. Williams, notes written 3 June–14 August 1944, Samuel T. Williams papers, Hoover Institute, Stanford University, Stanford, California.

3. Ibid.

4. Ibid.

5. Author's telephone interview and letter dated January 1986.

Chapter 2

1. Author's interview with Mr. and Mrs. Woodson Herbert Harris, Denton, Texas, October 1985.

2. *The Flashlight,* Denton High School, Denton, Texas, May 1916.

3. *The Bronco,* Denton High School Yearbook, Denton, Texas, 1916.

Chapter 3

1. Harrison, letter To Whom It May Concern, 10 July 1917.

2. Williams, letter to Lawrence Tarlton, 5 July 1957.

3. Hervey, quoted in the *San Antonio Express-News,* San Antonio, Texas, 27 May 1985.

4. Williams, speech to First Classmen, U.S. Military Academy, 8 May 1961, unpublished mimeograph sent to the author.

5. Author's interview with Col. Nathaniel Ward III, Hampton Roads, Virginia, April 1986.

6. Ibid.

Chapter 4

1. Williams, letter to the author, August 1977.

2. Williams, personal communication with the author, July 1976.

3. Paraphrased from Williams, "Co. I, 359th Infantry (90th Division) Near Pagny in the Moselle Valley, September 25–30, 1918," monograph written during 1930–31, U.S. Infantry School, Fort Benning, Georgia.

4. Ibid.

5. Williams, personal communication with the author, July 1976.

6. Ibid.

7. Williams, "Co. I."

8. Ibid.

9. Ibid.

10. Harris interview, October 1985.

Chapter 5

1. Williams, letter to Ida Williams Henderson, 11 January 1963.

2. Spear, letter to the author, 8 March 1988.

3. Cocheu, Academic Report, 1 June 1927, U.S. Army Infantry School, Fort Benning, Georgia.

4. Related by Williams to the author, 1976. Von Schell and Sam lost contact with each other after they completed the Infantry School Advance Course. However, while serving in Vietnam in 1959, Sam received a letter from Lt. Gen. Adolf Von Schell. In the letter, Von Schell told of his World War II experiences, one of which was having the responsibility for transporting German soldiers to Normandy after the Allied landings. He also told of being captured late in the war and sent to Poland for trial as a murderer, even though he had not been in Poland since 1915. Von Schell's release from the Polish authorities was gained by his wife Helene, who wrote to General Marshall and requested his assistance in getting Von Schell freed. Marshall knew Von Schell well and contacted Montgomery, who managed to have Von Schell returned to Germany from Poland, where he had been held for eighteen months without trial.

5. Williams, letter to Ida Williams Henderson, 11 January 1963.

Chapter 6

1. Excerpts are slightly edited for spelling and punctuation and are from the "90th Infantry Division Official After Action Operational Reports," Washington National Records Center, Washington, D.C.

2. Talbott, letter to the author, November 1985.

3. Author's interview with James O. Boswell, Minneapolis, Minnesota, 5 October 1985.

4. Author's interview with Eames Yates, Irving, Texas, 3–4 October 1987.

5. Author's interviews with Eames Yates, 1987, and Carl B. Everett, St. Louis, Missouri, October 1988.

6. Author's interview with Eames Yates, 1987.

7. Chester B. Hansen Diaries, 13 July 1944, U.S. Army Military History Institute (USAMHI), Carlisle Barracks, Pennsylvania.

Chapter 7

1. Omar N. Bradley, *A Soldier's Story* (New York: Henry Holt & Co., 1951), 299; 297

2. Undated folder, "Reminiscence of General Barth on Normandy," USAMHI, Carlisle Barracks, Pennsylvania.

3. Hansen Diaries; ibid.

4. Troy H. Middleton (with Frank James Price), *A Biography* (Baton Rouge: Louisiana State University Press, 1975), 183; ibid.

5. Hansen Diaries.

6. Author's interview with Eames Yates, 1987.

7. Bradley, *A Soldier's Story*, 297.

8. The Jacob W. Bealke Papers and Letters, USAMHI, Carlisle Barracks, Pennsylvania.

9. Hansen Diaries.

Chapter 8

1. The author's research of Army Ground Force (AGF) Inspector General files, AGF G3 Training Division Files, AGF History Files, and VIII Corps IG Training Reports did not reveal any red-tagging of the Ninetieth for training deficiencies. Research was conducted at the National Archives and at the Washington National Records Center by skilled, professional archivists.

2. Williams, memo to Lt. Gen. W.B. Smith, 3 August 1944.

3. Williams, letter to Capt. R.C. Couch, Jr., 13 October 1944.

4. James M. Gavin, *On to Berlin* (New York: Bantam, 1978), 233.

5. "Changing Army," oral history of Gen. William E. DePuy, "Senior Officer Oral History Program," USAMHI, Carlisle Barracks, Pennsylvania.

Chapter 9

1. Sutherland, letter to the author, 15 December 1985.

2. Ibid.

3. Related by Ted Dobol, author's interview, Fort Dix, New Jersey, April 1987.

4. Woolfley, letter to the author, 1 June 1986.

5. Colonel Williams, when he assumed command of the Twenty-sixth Infantry, also was appointed deputy commander of the Fürth-Nuremberg Enclave. A short time later, he was given the command of the Headquarters Command, International Military Tribunal, and then was further appointed commander of the Fürth-Nuremberg Enclave. He was held responsible for the administrative and operational efficiency of both elements. His combined command involved the morale and welfare of more than 10,000 officers and men. In October of 1946, he was awarded the Army Commenda-

tion Ribbon for his outstanding command ability.

6. Author's telephone interview with Ted Dobol, December 1985.

7. Statement to assembled Blue Spaders, Bamberg, Germany, December 1948.

Chapter 10

1. Williams, letter to Ida Williams Henderson, 18 January 1963.

2. Author's personal observation, Bamberg, Germany, September 1951.

3. Case, letter to the author, June 1985.

4. Mark Clark, *From the Danube to the Yalu* (New York: Harper & Brother's Publishers, 1954), 224.

5. Ibid.

6. Interview with Williams by William E. Sweet, 9 May 1975, "Senior Officer Oral History Program," USAMHI, Carlisle Barracks, Pennsylvania.

7. Ibid.

8. Maxwell Taylor, *Swords and Plowshares* (New York: W.W. Norton & Co., 1872), 145.

9. Sweet oral history interview.

Chapter 11

1. Williams oral history interview by Ted Gettinger, 1 March 1981, Lyndon Baines Johnson Library, Austin, Texas.

2. Author's interview with Williams, San Antonio, Texas, 1977.

3. Gettinger oral history interview.

4. Ibid.

5. Ibid.

6. Ibid.

7. Ibid.

8. Lt. Gen. Edward A. Partain wrote to the author in August 1985: "An interesting facet of [Sam's] character was the fact that in neither all male social gatherings and certainly never in mixed company did I ever hear him utter even the mildest of profanity or vulgarity. Yet I know from the year I spent with him in Korea that he could turn the air a blazing purple when he wanted."

9. Gettinger oral history interview.

10. General Williams' retirement orders credit him with "nearly forty-three years of active Federal Service." However, this author's records include a sheet completed by three officials of the Adjutant General's branch of the Department of the Army—Colbert, Horton, and Stewart—that credits General Williams with forty-four years, two months, and twenty-five days of active Federal Service for retirement purposes.

Selected Bibliography and Sources

American Battle Monuments Commission. *90th Division Summary of Operations in the World War.* Washington, D.C.: GPO, 1944.

————. *A Guide to the American Battlefields of Europe.* Washington, D.C.: GPO, 1927.

Blumenson, Martin. *Breakout and Pursuit.* United States Army in World War II. Washington, D.C.: Department of the Army, Office of the Chief of Military History, 1961.

Bradley, Gen. Omar N. *A Soldier's Story.* New York: Henry Holt and Co., 1951.

————, with Clay Blair. *A General's Life.* New York: Simon and Schuster, 1983.

Chester B. Hansen Diaries. U.S. Army Military History Institute, Carlisle Barracks, Pa.

Clark, Gen. Mark W. *From the Danube to the Yalu.* New York: Harper and Brothers Publishers, 1954.

Clay, Gen. Lucius D. *Decision in Germany.* Garden City: Doubleday and Co., 1950.

Crookenden, Napier. *Drop Zone Normandy.* New York: Charles Scribner's Sons, 1976.

Davis, Franklin M. *Come as a Conqueror*. New York: The Macmillan Co., 1967.

DePuy, Gen. William D. Interview. "Senior Officer Oral History Program," 1979. U.S. Army Military History Institute, Carlisle Barracks, Pa.

Dittmar, Gus C. *They Were First*. Austin: The Steck-Warlick Co., 1969.

DuPuy, Col. R. Ernest. *The Compact History of the United States Army*. New York: Hawthorn Books, Inc., 1956.

Emmett, Chris. *Give Way to the Right*. San Antonio: The Naylor Co., 1931.

"First U.S. Army, Report of Operations, 20 October 1943–1 August 1944." Washington, D.C.: GPO, n.d.

Forsythe, Lt. Gen. George I. Interview. "Senior Officer Oral History Program," 1974. U.S. Army Military History Institute, Carlisle Barracks, Pa.

Ganoe, William A. *The History of the United States Army*. 1940. Reprint. Ashton, Md.: Eric Lundberg, 1964.

Gavin, Gen. James M. *On to Berlin*. New York: Bantam Books, 1978.

Greenfield, Kent R., Robert R. Palmer, and Bell I. Wiley. *The Organization of Ground Combat Troops*. Washington, D.C.: Historical Division, Department of the Army, 1947.

Harmon, Maj. Gen. E.N. *Combat Commander*. Englewood Cliffs: Prentice-Hall, Inc., 1970.

Harrison, Gordon A. *Cross-Channel Attack*. United States Army in World War II. Washington, D.C.: Department of the Army, Office of the Chief of Military History, 1951.

A History of the 90th Division in World War II, 6 June 1944 to 9 May 1945. Baton Rouge: Army Navy Publishing Co.: 1946.

Hoyt, Edwin P. *The Invasion Before Normandy*. New York: Stein and Day, Publishers, 1985.

Jacob W. Bealke Papers and Letters. U.S. Army Military History Institute, Carlisle Barracks, Pa.

A Manual for Courts-Martial. Washington, D.C.: GPO, 1917.

Middleton, Troy H., with Frank James Price. *A Biography.* Baton Rouge: Louisiana State University Press, 1975.

Moss, Maj. James A. *Officer's Manual.* Menasha, Wisconsin: George Banta Publishing Co., 1917.

National Personnel Records Center, St. Louis, Mo. Samuel T. Williams file, including efficiency reports, reports of physical examinations, and assignments.

Omaha Beachhead. American Forces in Action. Washington, D.C.: Historical Division, War Department, 1945.

Palmer, Robert R., Bell I. Wiley, and William R. Keast. *The Procurement and Training of Ground Combat Troops.* United States Army in World War II. Washington, D.C.: Historial Division, Department of the Army, 1948.

"Reminiscence of General Barth on Normandy." Folder. U.S. Army Military History Institute, Carlisle Barracks, Pa.

Russell, Gordon. *The Army Almanac.* Harrisburg: Stackpole Co., 1959.

Spector, Ronald H. *Advice and Support: The Early Years 1941–1960.* Washington, D.C.: United States Army, Center of Military History, 1985.

Taylor, Maxwell. *Swords and Plowshares.* New York: W.W. Norton & Co., 1972.

U.S. Department of State, Office of the Historian. *Foreign Relations of the United States, 1955–1957,* Vol. 1. Washington, D.C.: GPO, 1985.

Utah Beach to Cherbourg. American Forces in Action. Washington, D.C.: Historical Division, Department of the Army, 1947.

Weigley, Russell F. *Eisenhower's Lieutenants.* 2 vols. Bloomington: Indiana University Press, 1981.

Williams, Samuel T. "Co. I, 359th Infantry (90th Division) Near Pagny in the Moselle Valley, September 25–30, 1918." Monograph written during 1930–31, U.S. Infantry School, Fort Benning, Ga.

———. Interview. "Senior Officer Oral History Program," 1975. U.S. Army Military History Institute, Carlisle Barracks, Pa.

———. Oral History Interview, 1981. Lyndon Baines Johnson Library, Austin, Tex.

———. Papers. Hoover Institute, Stanford University, Stanford, Calif.

Wythe, Maj. George. *A History of the 90th Division.* N.p.: 90th Division Association, 1920.

Index

H-Hour, 60, 62. *See also* Normandy, invasion
Halsey, Maj. Gen. M. B., 123, 124
Han River, 122
"Hanging Sam." *See* Williams, Samuel T.
Hansen, Lt. Col. Chet, 85
Harmon, Maj. Gen. Ernest N., 10–11, 102, 104, 105
Harris, General, 48–49
Harris, Lieutenant (aide to MacKelvie), 74
Harris, Woodson H., 158
Harrison, Capt. Sidney, 16, 20
Hartshorn, Dottie, 160–61
Hedgerows, 66, 76, 84; German defense in, 69, 82–83, 84–85, 96; *See also* Normandy, terrain
Henderson, Ida Williams (STW's sister), 5, 148
Hennen, Gen. Tom, 159
Hervey, Col. Stewart D.,22
Hill, Sgt. Paul D., 33, 39, 148
Ho Chi Minh, 138
Hodges, Mack B., 20
Hoffman, Luther, 20
Hokaido, 162
Hopkins, George M., 20
Hoss (STW's dog), 115, 148, 152, 159, 160
Hubner, Lt. Gen. Clarence R., 118
Hue, 139

Indochina, 137. *See also* Vietnam
Infantry Journal, 54
Infantry Officers Advance Course, 25
Interallied Games, 46
International Control Commission, 139
International Cooperation Administration, 141

Japan, 132
Jenkins, Lt. Gen. Ruben, 150
Jones, Capt. C. D., 30

Karhohs, Maj. Gen. Fred E., 151–54
Kean, Maj. Gen. William B., 93, 96, 97
Kilday, Lt. Col., 70, 77
Kingman, Col. Allen, 129
Kinheim, 41
Korea, 135, 138, 148, 166; conflict in122, 123, 125, 130, 132. *See also* Williams, Samuel T., in Korea

La Fière, 64, 68, 84
La Haye du Puits, 84, 89
La Hubert, 64
Landrum, Maj. Gen. Eugene M., 63, 64, 72, 79, 147; assumes command of Ninetieth, 73; ineffectiveness at Normandy, 73, 75–76, 87–88, 98–99; relief at Normandy, 88; seeks STW's reassignment and reduction, 91–92, 94–95, 97
Lansdale, Col. Ed., 136
Laos, 137, 139
Le Havre, 7
Le Mans, 46
Le Motey, 68
Lear, Lt. Gen. Ben, 83, 102–03
Leavenworth, Kans., 108, 112, 131, 147
Leon Springs, Tex, 19, 21–22, 27
Les Dupres, 65
Lessay, 84
Loutres, 64
Low Countries, 59
Ludwigsburg, 108
Luxembourg, 43

MAAG. *See* Military Assistance and Advisory Group
MacArthur, Gen. Douglas, 52, 122
MacKelvie, Brig. Gen. Jay W., 2–4, 60, 88; actions during Normandy invasion, 65, 67, 70–71, 74; assumes command of Ninetieth, 2–3; relief by Collins, 72–73
Mahlman line, 84–85, 86
Mann, Lt. Col. Carl, 130
Marathon, Battle of (490 B.C.), 24–25
Marshall, Gen. George C., 3, 99
McBroom, Col. W. S., 50
McCullough, John W., 21
McCormick, Miss, 14
McGee, Sen. Gail W., 143
McLain, Raymond S., 89
McNair, Lt. Gen. Lesley J., 21, 147
Merderet River, 60, 64, 65–66, 67, 68
Merriman, Mrs. George J., 158–59
Meuse River, 39, 121
Meuse–Argonne campaign, 40
Mexican bandits, 15–16, 17
Middleton, Maj. Gen. Troy H., 80, 86, 89, 91–92, 103; approves STW's reduction, 95–96
Milburn, Gen. Frank W., 112, 116, 124–25, 148, 166